I0156144

# TEACHER TELLS A STORY
## BOOK ONE

## Also by Rev. Jerome D. Hannan (1896-1965)

*(Co-authored with George Johnson and Sister M. Dominica)*

- **The Bible Story:** a textbook in biographical form for use of the lower grades of Catholic schools

- **Bible History:** a textbook of the Old and New Testaments for Catholic Schools

- **The Story of the Church, Her Founding, Mission and Progress:** a textbook in Church History

# Teacher Tells a Story

### Story-Lessons in Conduct and Religion

### By Rev. Jerome D. Hannan, D.D.

## Book One

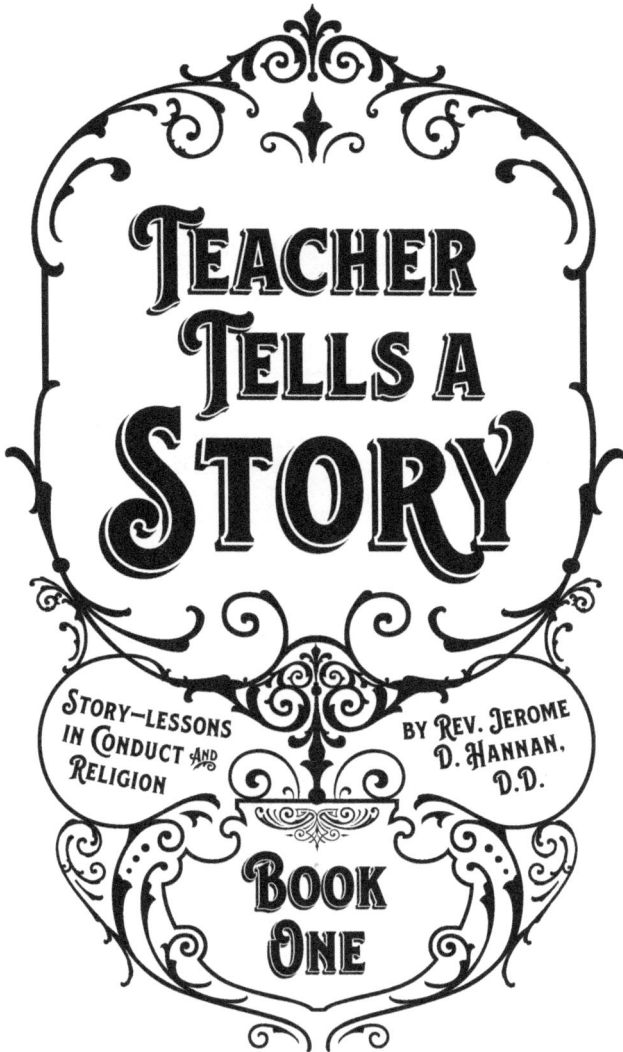

ST. AUGUSTINE ACADEMY PRESS
HOMER GLEN, ILLINOIS

Nihil Obstat

ARTHUR J. SCANLAN, S.T.D.
*Censor Librorum*

Imprimatur

✠ PATRICK, CARDINAL HAYES,
*Archbishop of New York*

NEW YORK, Oct. 22, 1925.

This book was originally published in 1925
by Benziger Brothers.

This facsimile edition was reproduced in 2023
by St. Augustine Academy Press.

ISBN: 978-1-64051-125-5

# PREFACE

Most writers on pedagogy are agreed that the teacher of the primary grades, and more particularly of the very first grade, requires a finer art and a higher technique for successful work than her confreres in the more advanced classes. She assumes charge of a group of boys and girls who are confronted with one of the first changes in their young lives, and to them it is a momentous change. Home and parent and all the varied interests of the family circle are not indeed entirely abandoned; but they are put aside for the first time during a large portion of the day. The children enter upon a new world: rows of desks, and the walls of the class-room, and the problems of school life, and the presence and guidance of a stranger—the teacher.

Whatever simple souls and pious faddists may assert, actual experience, embedded in the memory of men and women, attests that normal children do not like to go to school. Books read with avidity outside of school are often distasteful in the class-room; projects and problems that are attacked with the keenest delight in the home or on the playgrounds are frequently lacking in appeal when presented by the teacher. Young America is willing indeed to work, and usually realizes what is good for him, but he is ill at ease and is inclined to rebel under the discipline and the enforced tasks of this new world of the school.

The primary teacher has the opportunity and the responsibility of introducing the young boy and girl into this new and strange world. Much of the success and failure of training in the higher grades will be traceable to her work and methods. She is confronted not with *tabulae rasae* to be written upon at her own whim; not with inert pieces of clay to be moulded in the light of her more mature experience; but with minds that are very alert, with imaginations that are extremely vivid, with bodies that are bundles of energy, and with souls that are keenly sensitive to impressions from the outside world. If the primary teacher realizes her responsibility and opportunity she will make her chief concern, not school subjects, but the children of her class-room; she will teach, not arithmetic, grammar and spelling, but her boys and girls.

Modern pedagogy has provided her with very admirable weapons for her task. Her greatest help of a general nature will perhaps be found in the application of the universal doctrine of interest. This principle is applied in the class-room by means of a great variety of devices; perhaps the most serviceable of them is that of story-telling.

Dr. Hannan's "Teacher Tells a Story" will be a welcome addition to the armory of the Catholic primary teacher. Her field embraces all the problems of her colleague in the secular school, and adds the fundamental and difficult task of teaching religion.

It is a truism to state that the teaching of religion, with all that term implies, is the main purpose of the Catholic school. It should be equally true to assert that it is the best taught subject in that school. Experience shows that such is not the case. The class in religion frequently degenerates into a verbatim recital of catechetical questions and answers. The theological treatise is shorn of some of its abstruse terminology, and presented to the young mind of the grade pupil who instinctively shuns abstractions and delights in concrete realities. Catholic educators are fully alive to this abnormality and are endeavouring to provide our teachers with suitable remedies. Teacher's manuals are being published which embody the sound and tested principles of pedagogy and assist the teacher to apply them to the teaching of religion. They adjust the religious truth to the capacity of the learner and they employ language adapted to the child's intelligence; they arouse and sustain the interest of the child in the religious lesson; they provide for assimilation of the religious truth and make it real, they call for expression, not merely by a repetition of words conned by rote, but by means of oral and written expression in the pupil's own words, as a test that to some real extent he has grasped and assimilated the religious truth.

Dr. Hannan's work is a valuable addition to this growing literature and will be given a hearty welcome by Catholic teachers in the primary grades.

The stories embodied in the Manual are not the result of a theoretical interest in this very important field; they are the fruit of experience in the class-room. They have been tried and tested. They formed part of the author's work in teaching religion in the elementary grades of a large city school. At the solicitation of primary teachers, they were issued in mimeographed form and were used for several years by experienced teachers. The children found them an unending source of interest. A simple, but striking, religious truth was borne home by each story in words they could easily grasp and in a manner that left a lasting impression on their young minds and hearts. The stories were dramatized by groups of boys and girls both in school and at home, and in several instances the parents of the children applied to the teacher for copies of the book.

As a result of this experience extending over several

8 PREFACE

years, Dr. Hannan was persuaded to publish the book in its present form as a teacher's manual. The Superintendent of Parish Schools of the Diocese of Pittsburgh can attest that for the past three years he has heard the stories told by the teacher and repeated and dramatized by the pupils. The teachers who have used the work in its original form are agreed that it aided them in the teaching of religion; that it captivated the hearts of the children was proved by their clamoring to be permitted to tell one of the stories and by their insistence on being permitted to make their own selection; parents have told of the stories repeated at home for their benefit and edification.

"Teacher Tells a Story" is not an experiment. It has proved its worth in the primary grades of a large diocesan school system. In the light of that experience, we feel that it will be welcomed by primary teachers everywhere, who will find in it suitable material and a proper method for leading their young charges to the knowledge and practice of their religion and to the love and service of Jesus Christ.

R. L. HAYES, D.D.

*Superintendent of Parish Schools,*
  *Diocese of Pittsburgh.*

# CONTENTS

## PART ONE

Story-Lessons in Conduct and Religion

### I. INTEREST IN SCHOOL.*

### II. COOPERATION WITH THE TEACHER.

* For the convenience of the teacher the general division of the subject matter is indicated here. See Introduction, page 19, for fuller details and explanation of sequence.

9

## VI. THE LORD'S PRAYER.

## VII. THE HAIL MARY.

## VIII. THE OMNIPOTENCE OF GOD.

## IX. THE HOLY TRINITY.

## X. THE CONFITEOR.

## XI. THE RESURRECTION.

## XII. THE DESCENT OF THE HOLY GHOST.

## XIII. HOLY COMMUNION.

## XIV. CONFESSION.

## APPENDIX TO PART ONE.

## PART TWO

### Teachers' Helps

# INTRODUCTION

THE catechetical system that is proposed here for the service of teachers engaged in conveying the truths of religion to the minds of children in the first grade is an evolution from a series of stories presented by the author to the minds of children in that grade. They were very successful when proposed to the children by him. Still, as differences in training and differences in modes of thinking are to be found among teachers, it is thought advisable to set down for the benefit of those who may be interested in using this system, the logical connection that exists between the stories, as well as the doctrines illustrated and taught by them.

## Division of Subject Matter

There are one hundred and eighty-two stories. The idea is to provide the teacher with one story for every day in the school year. The first point dwelt upon in them is the necessity of sacrificing one's love for home during the hours spent in school. Stories numbered one to fourteen deal with this, introducing the example of our divine Saviour, who left home to save us, as well as the Sign of the Cross which is the symbol of that Redemption. The fourteenth story is a review of what has been taught in the preceding stories.

Stories numbered fifteen to twenty-three inclusive take up for the child unused to school life the necessity of cooperating with the teacher, principally through silence in speech and movement. The example of Christ assisting Saint Joseph to flee into Egypt is held before the minds of the children, and they are shown that it was through silence that Herod's soldiers were prevented from detecting where the divine Child was. The twenty-third story is a review of the stories that have preceded it on this subject.

Stories numbered twenty-four to twenty-nine inclusive have to do with the cooperation of the children among themselves. Here the marching in the Holy Name Procession is held out as an example of the cooperation necessary in leaving school. Story twenty-nine reviews what has gone before it on the same topic.

Stories thirty to thirty-six inclusive use the knowledge of the teacher's authority and ability to convey to the child mind the fact that God is also a teacher, that He knows everything, and that we can learn from Him whatever He chooses to reveal to us.

The transition is then made to prayer. Stories thirty-seven to forty-five inclusive show first that we can expect nothing but evil from the devil but that God will give us everything that is good for us if we ask Him in the proper way. The forty-fifth story is a review of the stories that are presented before it, dealing with the same matter.

From prayer in general we pass to prayer in particular and take up the Lord's Prayer. Stories forty-six to seventy-five inclusive deal with the Lord's Prayer. Stories forty-six and forty-seven deal with the first clause; stories forty-eight to fifty-one inclusive, with the second; stories fifty-two and fifty-three, with the third; stories fifty-four to fifty-six inclusive, with the fourth; stories fifty-seven to fifty-nine inclusive, with the fifth. The sixth is skipped because it was treated under the heading of prayer in general, particularly in the forty-first story. Stories sixty to sixty-three inclusive consider the seventh clause; sixty-four to sixty-eight inclusive, the eighth; sixty-nine to seventy-four inclusive, the last. In the last series it is shown that though physical evil is sometimes a thing resulting in moral good, we are always glad to be saved from it by God. Story seventy-five is a story reviewing the whole of the Lord's Prayer.

The next stories deal with the Hail Mary. This is taken up in stories seventy-six to eighty-nine inclusive. In order to deal with the Hail Mary intelligently it was necessary to introduce an explanation of what the angels are; otherwise the children would not know who Gabriel was. Similarly, it was found necessary to describe the relationship of John the Baptist to our Lord in order that the child might understand the reason for the Blessed Virgin's visit to her cousin, Elizabeth. Stories seventy-six to seventy-nine deal with the angel's salutation; eighty to eighty-three inclusive, with the greeting of Saint Elizabeth; eighty-four to eighty-eight inclusive, with our petition to Mary. Story eighty-nine reviews the Hail Mary.

Here we introduce another of God's attributes, that of Omnipotence. The children have already learned that God knows everything; here they learn that He can do all things. Incidentally the children are taught that God made them for a specific end, that end is explained to them, and the means to obtain it suggested. All this is found in stories ninety to ninety-six inclusive.

Previously when dealing with the Sign of the Cross it was insinuated that there are three Persons in God. Here in stories ninety-seven to one hundred inclusive, a more explicit account of the Trinity is given the children.

We skip the Apostles' Creed as involving doctrinal matters beyond the grasp of first-grade children, and consider the Confiteor. This takes up the matter in stories one hundred and one to one hundred eleven. It was found necessary to explain to the children who Saint Michael the Archangel is. They heard about Saint John the Baptist, in stories eighty and eighty-one. They know as yet nothing about Saints Peter and Paul; so the identity of these two Apostles must be made clear to them. Story one hundred eleven reviews the Confiteor.

So far the children have become acquainted with the Unity and Trinity of God, the Incarnation and Death of Christ. Nothing has been said about the Resurrection and the Descent of the Holy Ghost on Pentecost. These are considered in stories one hundred twelve to one hundred twenty-three. The institution of the Sacrament of Penance during the sojourn of our Saviour on earth after the Resurrection is introduced in story one hundred nineteen. Story one hundred twenty-three is a review of what has preceded on this topic.

As the children of this grade are usually prepared for the reception of their first Holy Communion at the end of the year, the rest of the stories deal with confession and Communion. Holy Communion is taken up first, and is dealt with in stories one hundred twenty-four to one hundred forty-five.

The institution of the Sacrament takes up the matter in stories one hundred twenty-four to one hundred thirty-seven; the reception of Holy Communion frequently, and visits to the Blessed Sacrament, as means of warding off temptation are insisted upon in stories one hundred thirty-eight to one hundred forty-five inclusive.

Stories from one hundred forty-five to the end deal with confession. Confession of sins and sorrow are stressed. Examination of conscience, and the need for divine help in that examination are also explained. The third, fifth, seventh, and eighth commandments of God, and the Friday precept of the church, are explained in stories one hundred seventy-four to one hundred seventy-eight. The second commandment was explained before in the stories dealing with the Holy Name Procession and the explanation of "Hallowed be Thy Name," in the Lord's Prayer. The fourth commandment has been stressed in practically all the stories depicting the commission of sin. The prime duty of the child's state in life, of course, demanded this.

From what has been said, then, these stories have been shown to deal with the Unity and Trinity of God, the Incarnation, Death, and Resurrection of the Second Person; the Descent of the Third Person on the Apostles. They show God's Omnipotence, Omniscience, Mercy, Love, Providence, and Eternity. They explain that God will reward the good and punish the wicked. They tell what the reward of the good is. They teach that God is the Creator of all things. They point to man's dignity and the special end God had in creating Him. They treat at great length of the Sacraments of Penance and Holy Eucharist. They give the children an idea of all the commandments of God, with the exception of the sixth and ninth. They inculcate the necessity of sacrifice, cooperation, charity, and obedience.

From the life of our Saviour we introduce the motive that caused Him to leave His home in Heaven; the Annunciation; His flight into Egypt; His being preceded by John the Baptist; the changing of water into wine; the prophecy about the rebuilding the temple; the cure of the two blind men; the cure of the lunatic; the calming of the storm at sea; the feeding of the multitude with the loaves and fishes; the Last Supper; the carrying of the Cross; the death on the Cross; the Resurrection; the institution of the Sacrament of Penance; the Ascension.

Regarding the foundation of the Church we note that attention is paid to the institution of the two Sacraments, Penance and Holy Eucharist; that the Descent of the Holy Ghost on the Apostles is described; the constitution of the college of Apostles is indicated; Peter's headship is pointed out; Paul's conversion is described; his intrepid journeying for the faith is taught.

While the stories seem to be written out in full, we must assure the teacher that they represent the minimum of detail that can be told the pupil, if success is to be obtained. The individual teacher should enlarge on the details surrounding the point in each. Both descriptive and narrative details that are not too far away from the point and that serve to sustain interest, will be apropos.

The writer has appended a list of questions to each story, that will serve as a kind of catechism, demanding from the children not merely static and memorized, but dynamic and intelligent, answers that will show whether or not they understand what has been taught them. Again, the teacher is urged to ask many more questions that her ingenuity may suggest. The questions given are merely to act as guides to show what type of question ought to be asked. A plan for more detailed development of the stories is outlined in the Appendix (p. 149).

There has been added, moreover, a Topical Index. It is thought that this may help the teacher when she is striving to find a story out of course. For example, she may be intent upon driving home the necessity of forgiving one's enemy, and this late in the year. She may forget what story dealt with that point. The Topical Index will refer her to stories numbered sixty to sixty-three, inclusive.

The purpose of Part Two, and its relation to the supplementary reader, "Religion Hour: Book One" is sufficiently explained in the Preface (p. 159).

This Foreword was inspired by the author's thought that she who is to teach these stories should receive from him all the help it is possible for him to give in writing. It is hoped that what is said here will achieve that purpose.

If only one teacher succeeds in proposing these stories to her class in a way that will make the children use their minds, and not their memories alone, the writer will feel that the time spent in preparing them was not lost.

# PART ONE
## STORY-LESSONS IN CONDUCT AND RELIGION

# TO AROUSE INTEREST IN SCHOOL

## 1. The Bee That Wouldn't Leave Home

I am sure that all my little friends know what a bee does. Why! a bee makes honey! But before the bee can make honey it must fly away from its home to the pretty flowers and gather honey there. There was one time a naughty little bee that wouldn't leave home to gather honey like the rest. The other bees didn't like that. They warned Mr. Bee that something dreadful would happen if he would not work with them. He paid no attention to them. One day, the farmer who owned the bees came out to look at them. He found Mr. Bee stung to death. I wonder who did it and why?

*Questions:* 1—Why didn't Mr. Bee gather honey like the other bees? 2—How could he have saved himself from being punished? 3—What will happen to little boys and girls who will not leave home to go to school?

## 2. Thomas Smith, the Dunce

I suppose, children, that when I told you of the foolish bee, you thought no boy or girl would act like that. Thomas Smith, though, was a little boy of six years who did not want to leave home to go to school. He cried, and cried, and cried. At last, his mother allowed him to stay home. Daddy kept on telling him that he would never know anything if he wouldn't go to school. He found out his mistake pretty soon. All his friends were learning to read and write and he couldn't. One day he ran and coaxed his mother to let him go to school.

"I don't want to be a dunce," he cried.

Mother was delighted, you can bet.

*Questions:* 1—Did Thomas Smith do wrong in not obeying mother? 2—Do you think that Thomas was brave or cowardly? 3—Why was Thomas' mother delighted?

### 3. Mary Murphy's Dream

Mary Murphy was a little girl of six and a half years. She didn't want to start to school either. One night before school started, she dreamed she was at a moving picture show. She saw there a schoolroom. A Sister was teaching the little boys and girls. At first she couldn't tell who the Sister was but when the Sister turned around she saw it was herself.

Then while she dreamed, she heard a voice whisper, "Mary, that's what you will be if you go to school."

Did Mary go to school? I'd rather let you, dear children, answer that.

*Questions:* 1—Do you think that Mary liked the Sisters? 2—Who do you think whispered to Mary while she was asleep? 3—Would you like to be what Mary wanted to be?

### 4. James Kelly and the Street Cleaner

It's strange, dear children, how I found out about so many children who didn't want to go to school but who changed their minds because they didn't want to be dunces. I want to tell you about another boy of whom I heard. James Kelly just knew he'd be homesick for his mama if he went to school. One day as he was sitting on the curb in front of his home the man who cleans the streets came along with his little wagon.

James told him all about his trouble. The man began to cry.

"Oh! you foolish boy!" said he. "Do you want to be forced to work like me? Wouldn't you rather be a doctor or a priest? Well, if you would, you'll have to go to school."

James was glad he talked to the poor man. After that there was no more trouble about James' going to school.

*Questions:* 1—Do you think a boy really loves mother who won't leave home to go to school because he thinks he will be homesick? 2—Did James do right in talking to the street-cleaner? Why? 3—How would you answer the questions the man asked James?

## 5. The Raindrop

You have heard about little children who left home to go to school because they wanted to become great. Dear children, did you ever hear of anyone leaving home because he wanted to help other people? That was just what a little raindrop I heard of was willing to do. You know that the things we eat need water to grow. One time in a country not far away everything was withering because there was no rain. The people saw their food drying up and they knew they would have to starve if no rain came. So they prayed for rain. And God told the raindrop to come down with many of his friends. He obeyed and saved the people's food for them. Like God the Son, the raindrop came down to earth to make boys and girls happy.

*Questions:* 1—What did the raindrop do for God? 2—What did the raindrop do for the people? 3—Would you want to leave home for the reason the raindrop left?

N. B.—For teachers' helps see page 163.

## 6. A Brother's Farewell

"Please, Thomas, do not go. Don't you love your sister? Why must you go far away across the big ocean in a ship to that country where I shall never see you again?"

Thomas was only a young man, just twenty-three years old. But he answered bravely, "Because, dear sister, I must save the souls of men who do not know about God."

Thomas was going away from home to China to tell the poor Chinese about God and to help them get to Heaven. He was not thinking about being great. He was leaving home to help others.

*Questions:* 1—What is the difference between Thomas in this story and Thomas Smith? 2—Is Thomas like the raindrop in any way? 3—How is Thomas' purpose different from the raindrop's?

## 7. The Teaser

Frank Brown was not a Catholic. He was only six years old. He liked to tease Catholic boys and girls. He would laugh at them for going to church on Sunday and for not eating meat on Friday. One day he saw little Michael Sweeney passing a Catholic church. Michael lifted his cap. Maybe Frank wasn't glad he saw that!

"Oh ho!" he teased, "Michael Sweeney tips his hat to an old stone building."

"I guess that's all you know about it," said Michael. "I'm not tipping my hat to an old stone building."

"Well, what are you tipping it for, then?" asked Frank.

"Will you give me a ride on your bike, if I tell you?" said Michael. Frank promised he would, but just then

Michael's mother called him and he could not tell Frank about it until the next day.

*Questions:* 1—Would you tease people like Frank Brown did? 2—Would you get angry if anyone treated you as Frank treated Michael? 3—Did Michael do right in promising to tell Frank why he tipped his cap?

## 8. God's House

Michael Sweeney was only seven years old but I tell you he was smart for that age. He knew enough to tell Frank Brown why he tipped his hat on passing a Catholic church. The reason he gave him was this.

"Because God is there on the altar and I say, 'How do you do?' to Him."

Frank was astonished.

"Do you mean to tell me God leaves Heaven to come and stay on your old altar?" he asked.

"Our altar is not an old altar, Frank Brown. I guess if it's good enough for God, it's not an old altar. And God really is there. We can't see Him there. There was a time, though, when people could see Him walking and talking with men. And He left home, His home in Heaven, just for us."

Michael began to tell how God came down on earth, but his story is so long that we'll tell about it tomorrow.

*Questions:* 1—Could you have answered Frank before you heard this story? 2—What was Michael's answer to Frank? 3—Does the story of the raindrop make you think of God leaving home? 4—What other story you have heard makes you think of it?

N. B.—For teachers' helps see page 167.

## 9. Leaving a Home in Heaven

Michael Sweeney had heard from his teacher the story of how the raindrop came down to save the people from starving. He told that story to Frank Brown. Then he said that as the raindrop had come down to save, so God had come down from His home in Heaven to save us from the fire of Hell.

"Just think how you'd hate to leave your home to go to a place where you were going to be insulted, just to help other people. That's what God did."

"I never knew that," said Frank.

"Well, don't you think I have a right to tip my cap to God after doing that for me?"

"Sure I do," answered Frank, "and I'm going to do it, too."

Michael had helped Frank to love God.

*Questions:* 1—Did the people thank God for leaving Heaven for them? 2—Will you be rewarded for leaving home for school? 3—How are you following God's example when you come to school?

## 10. Funny Motions

"Catherine, why do you make those funny motions with your hands when you pass your church?" This was the question Grace Hawkins asked Catherine McCullough, her neighbor and friend.

"Funny motions! Why, Grace, I'm surprised at you. They're not funny motions. I make the Sign of the Cross when I pass the church to honor Our Lord who is on the altar in it."

"That's the first time I ever heard of such a thing," answered Grace. "Is it hard to do? My! How I wish you would show me how!"

"I shall show you if you promise me that you won't make fun of it."

"Honestly, I shan't make fun of it. Please show me, won't you?"

And Catherine commenced to instruct Grace. What she did we shall find out tomorrow.

*Questions:* 1—Where did Catherine say Our Lord is? 2—Why do you think she did right in telling Grace that? 3—Do you think Grace was bad or just ignorant?

### 11. Our Badge

Catherine McCullough explained to Grace Hawkins that a cross is made by putting two boards, or two sticks, or two lines across one another. In just the same way we make the Sign of the Cross. We draw two make-believe lines across each other, one from the forehead to the breast, and the other from the left to the right shoulder.

"I hope you know which is your left shoulder," she said to Grace.

Grace tried to make the Sign of the Cross. At first she touched the right shoulder before the left, but soon she could make the lines as well as Catherine.

"There are certain words to be said when you make those lines," explained Catherine, "but we'll learn them tomorrow or the next day."

*Questions:* 1—How do you make a cross? 2—What is the cross a sign of? 3—What actions do you use when you make the Sign of the Cross?

### 12. The Holy Trinity

Grace would not allow Catherine to wait a whole day before telling her the words to be said in making the Sign of the Cross. She came over to see Catherine the same night and begged her to finish the lesson. Catherine was glad that she was so interested.

"Well," she said, "when you touch your forehead you

say, 'In the name of the Father;' then, touching your breast you say, 'and of the Son;' when you touch your left shoulder you say, 'and of the Holy Ghost;' and you end by touching the right shoulder and saying, 'Amen.' "

It took a little while for Grace to be able to say the words and do the actions at the same time. Soon she was able to make the Sign of the Cross perfectly. She was so proud that she ran right home to show her daddy and mother what she had learned.

*Questions:* 1—Was Grace anxious to learn what words to say in making the Sign of the Cross? 2—Are you as anxious as Grace to learn them? 3—What words do you say in making the Sign of the Cross?

## 13. The Cross on the Locket

Rose Hoffman received a beautiful locket with a cross from her daddy for her birthday present. You all know what a Catholic little girl would think of such a wonderful present. She was proud of it and wore it outside to show her little friends the very day daddy gave it to her. Soon one naughty girl laughed at her for wearing a cross. Rose was not afraid.

"I'm glad to wear it to show Our Lord I thank Him for dying on it for me," she answered.

The little girl was so ashamed that she asked Rose to forgive her. Rose said she would. She also told her all about how God came down on earth, leaving His home in Heaven, to be nailed on the cross, just because He loved us. The story made the naughty little girl take the cross and kiss it.

*Questions:* 1—Why do people wear crosses on their coats or on lockets? 2—Did Rose help the naughty little girl?

How? 3—Who do you think was brighter, Michael Sweeney or Rose Hoffman?

N. B.—For teachers' helps see page 171.

### 14. Patrick McCaffrey's Reason

Three little boys stood outside the school gate one day talking about school, and why they were glad to leave mother and daddy for a few hours every day to come to school.

"I don't want to be a dunce," said John Roach, "that's why I'm coming to school."

"And I," said Philip O'Reilly, "want to make a great man of myself, a doctor, or a priest, or something like that."

"But I," said Patrick McCaffrey, "am glad to leave home to come to school for the same reason that God was glad to leave His home to come on earth—to help others. The more I know, the more I can help other people. And when it gets hard for me to study, I'm just going to think of the cross and see God dying on it and say, 'Patrick, studying is not as hard as that.' I want to help others as God did."

I think Patrick's reason was the best.

*Questions:* 1—What story does John Roach's reason remind you of? 2—What story does Philip O'Reilly's reason remind you of? 3—Why is Patrick McCaffrey's reason the best?

## II. COOPERATION WITH THE TEACHER

### 15. The Team of Horses

You know what a team of horses is—two horses helping each other to pull the same wagon. One time there were two horses named Bill and Sam, whose owner used them to pull the same wagon. Both were strong; both were beautiful. Bill, however, was a white horse and was liked most by the children, who fed him apples, but gave Sam none. Sam became jealous. He made up his mind one night that he would not help Bill to pull any more. The next day as they were pulling a big load of potatoes, Sam quit pulling. Bill pulled the wagon about a square but could go no farther. The owner saw that Sam was not pulling, so he whipped Sam until he commenced to do his work again.

*Questions:* 1—Can you have the heavier wagon pulled by one or by two horses? 2—Did the children hurt Sam? If they didn't why was he jealous? 3—Did the owner of the team do right in whipping Sam?

## 16. Sam's Punishment

Sam helped Bill to pull after being whipped, but Mr. Scanlon, who was his owner, decided to get rid of him. He thought to himself that Sam might refuse to pull some day when he was crossing the railroad track, and so make Bill and the wagon and everyone on it be hit by the train. So Sam was sold to an old rag man who gave him only one meal of hay a day, gave him an old dirty stall to live in, and made him work three times as long as he had to work before. All this because he would not work with Bill and help him to pull the heavy load.

*Questions:* 1—What might Sam's jealousy have made him do? 2—Do children do bad things if they get jealous? 3—Do jealous people deserve Sam's punishment? Why?

## 17. A Helping Hand

Terence McShane was a little boy of only seven years, but he had a very kind heart. One day just after he had begun to go to school he was walking home. He was looking out at the crossings just as his mother had told him to do, when he saw an old woman standing over a basket of groceries which she had set down on the sidewalk. The woman was crying. The basket was so heavy she could not carry it any farther. Terry wondered if he could help. He knew he wasn't very strong. He told the old woman he would take hold of one side of the handle, if she would hold the other. And what do you think?—the old woman was able to carry it with Terry's help. Together they got the basket home to the old lady's house.

*Questions:* 1—Was Terence McShane obedient to his mother? How? 2—Do you think it was hard to help carry the basket? 3—Why did Terence help the poor woman?

N. B.—For teachers' helps see page 175.

## 18. Terry's Reward

When Terry left the basket on the lady's kitchen table, she gave him a nickel for helping her. He was just going to leave the house when he bumped into Father Connors, the priest at Terry's church.

"What are you doing here?" he asked Terry.

The old lady told Father Connors what Terry had done.

"So you did that for my mother," said Father Connors, "I'm going to say a Mass for you. But that's not all, I am going to be your friend for life, Terry. If you ever need anything at all, just ask me for it."

That was Terry's reward.

*Questions:* 1—Do you think Terence helped the poor woman for the money she gave him? Would you like him if he did? 2—Why do you think Father Connors was so pleased? 3—

Which reward would you rather have, Father Connors' or the one his mother gave Terence?

## 19. Simon of Cyrene

Many, many years ago the devil told the Jews to kill Christ. You know already that Christ was God, that He had left His home in Heaven to come down to save you and me from Hell, and to help us get to Heaven. Well the devil was so mad to think he was losing us that he whispered to the Jews that they ought to kill Christ. So they listened to him and made a big, heavy cross—almost as big as a telegraph pole, and just as heavy—and made Him carry it up a big hill, intending to nail Him on it. But it was so heavy He fell three times. The Jews thought sure He would die before they reached the top of the hill. They did not want Him to die that way. They wanted to nail Him to the Cross. So they made a traveler who was standing watching the procession take one end of the Cross. That man's name was Simon. At first he did not want to help Our Lord. After a little while, though, he was glad they picked on him. For helping Him carry the Cross, Our Lord was good to Simon and made him His friend; and you may be sure Our Lord takes good care of His friends in Heaven.

*Questions:* 1—Why was the devil angry with Our Lord for leaving Heaven? 2—Would you have wanted to help Our Lord if you had seen Him carrying that heavy Cross? 3—Do you have any cross to carry now, for Our Lord?

## 20. Escaping from Herod

When Our Lord came down on earth He came as a little Baby. There was a wicked King living at that time who wanted to kill this little Baby. That King was Herod. He was afraid that this Baby would grow up and be King instead of one of his own children. So he sent a lot of soldiers to kill Him. But an angel spoke to St. Joseph in his sleep, and St. Joseph got up and took Our Lord and ran away from the old King. And Our Lord, even though He seemed to be just a little baby, did not cry. He had to leave His bed in the middle of the night, but He did not cry. If He had cried, the soldiers would have found Him. So by keeping quiet, He really *helped* St. Joseph to save Him.

*Questions:* 1—Was Our Lord a big man from the time He came down on earth? 2—Who was jealous of Him when He was just a little Baby? 3—Did Our Lord have to do anything to help St. Joseph to save Him from the wicked King?

## 21. Jane Gray's Mistake

Jane Gray was a little girl of six and a half years who had just begun school in September. At home she had been used to talking whenever she liked. Many times she even made her mother sick by the noise she made, hammering on pans, ringing bells, and the like. When she came to school she thought she could continue doing the same thing. She commenced to talk to the children in front of her, in back of her, and beside her. She tapped her pencil on her desk so loud that the other children could not hear what Sister had to say. All the other children thought she was terribly bad. One little girl even said she wished Jane's mother would keep her home because no one could learn anything with all the talking she did and all the noise she made.

*Questions:* 1—Do people who make noise like Jane imitate Our Lord? 2—Does God like noisy people? 3—Why will you not be like Jane?

## 22. Mr. Gray's Advice

One day Jane was sitting by her father's side. She told him about the bad horse, Sam; and about Terry McShane helping the old lady with the groceries; and about the man that helped Our Lord to carry the Cross; and about Our Lord helping St. Joseph to escape by not crying.

"I hope," said her daddy, "that you have learned the lesson of those stories."

"Why," said Jane, "I don't know whom to help."

"You can help your Sister to teach the little boys and girls."

"How can I do that? I do not know enough."

"Oh!" said her daddy, "don't you know Our Lord helped St. Joseph to escape with Him just by keeping quiet and not crying? That is the way you can help Sister, by keeping from talking and making noise."

Jane felt ashamed of herself for what she had done before, and made up her mind she was not going to act that way any more.

*Questions:* Do you think Jane learned anything from the stories she told her daddy? Have you? What? 2—Why do you think Jane's daddy was a real, good daddy? 3—If your daddy told you what Jane's daddy told her, would you be angry or would you thank him? Why?

## 23. Helping Teacher

Margaret Flynn had listened intently to the stories of people helping one another. She did not like Sam because he was so mean in refusing to help Bill pull the heavy wagon. She thought he deserved the punishment he received. She was delighted to hear of the kindness of Terence McShane and she thought that

Father Connors must have been very pleased to find that Terence had treated his mother so well. She could not understand how Simon of Cyrene would refuse to help Our Lord carry His Cross. She knew that she would be anxious to do it. Of course, when she heard that Our Lord did not cry when He was being taken to Egypt, she was not surprised. That was just what she expected Him to do because He was God. But the story she liked best of all was the one which told how Mr. Gray advised his daughter to be silent in school and so help Sister. She was glad that she had helped her Sister to teach herself and the rest of the class.

*Questions:* 1—Tell me some people you have heard of in the stories I told who were helpful to others. 2—Do you know any friends of yours who help others? 3—Which of the stories spoken of by Margaret Flynn do you like best and why?

## III. COOPERATION WITH OTHER PUPILS

### 24. The Toy Soldiers

Ruth Jones was playing with her brother's tin soldiers. She had them arranged in the funniest way. No one ever saw soldiers marching the way she had them placed. You know soldiers march in straight lines, but Ruth had them placed in all kinds of crooked lines. You know also that they keep the same distance away from each other. The way Ruth had them placed you would think some were walking on the heels of others. Her brother, Robert, came in while she had them arranged this way.

"Oh! what an ugly army!" he laughed.

Ruth was angry with him, but she watched him while he arranged them. When he was through they were all arranged in lines, with equal distances between them. Ruth had to tell her brother that now they looked ever so much better.

*Questions:* 1—What was wrong with Ruth's arrangement of the toy soldiers? 2—Does it make any difference how real soldiers march in parade? 3—If you had been Ruth, could you have arranged the soldiers properly after watching her brother?

N. B.—For teachers' helps see page 180.

### 25. The Holy Name Parade

Virginia Bell went with her mother to see the Holy Name Parade. She was only seven years old but she knew that the men were marching in the parade to honor the name of Our Lord, that they were marching to teach other men not to swear. Her mother selected a nice spot where she could see the whole procession, and where she could see her daddy well. Virginia watched the whole procession and when her daddy came along she waved, and waved, and waved. Daddy smiled at her and walked on. They waited until the whole procession was over and then started for their home.

"I think the men from our Church looked the best," said Virginia.

"And why?" asked her mother.

"Because they kept their lines straight, and they walked together, keeping step with one another."

"Tell that to your daddy when he comes home," advised Virginia's mother, "and we may have ice cream for dinner."

*Questions:* 1—Why do men march in the Holy Name Procession? 2—Why do you think men ought to march well in it? 3—Did Virginia's daddy march well? Why?

## 26. Mr. Bell's Treat

Virginia could scarcely wait until her daddy came home to tell him how well he had marched. When he came into the house she threw herself into his arms and kissed him.

"If there had been any prizes for the best marchers," said Virginia, "I'm sure the men from our Church would have won the first."

Daddy was anxious to see why Virginia thought they had marched well.

"Because," said she, "you kept in line, kept your heads high, and kept step with one another."

"I am glad you know so much about marching," said her daddy, "and just because you have been so nice about it, we'll have to call up for some ice cream for dinner."

Was Virginia happy? You had better answer that.

*Questions:* 1—Do you make daddy as happy as Virginia did? 2—Do you know as much about marching as she? Show me. 3—Can we make ourselves happy by pleasing others? How?

## 27. Virginia's Marching

After dinner, Mr. Bell called Virginia to his side and said to her.

"Virginia, you thought we marched well, today. I am glad you watched so closely. But I am going to ask you a question. How do you march? Do you keep in line, and hold your head high, and keep step?"

"Why I never marched in my life," said Virginia.

"Oh! just think! you march sometimes, too. I'm sure you do."

Virginia guessed, and guessed, but finally had to give up. She knew of no time when she had marched.

"Why, how do you come out of school? You come out in ranks, don't you? Don't you call that marching?"

"I'm afraid I don't," answered Virginia, "because I know I do not walk as straight and keep such good step as you."

"But don't you think you ought to?" asked Mr. Bell.

"I know I ought, and I'm going to, after this," replied his daughter.

*Questions:* 1—If Mr. Bell had asked you how you march, what would you answer? 2—Are you going to imitate soldiers in marching? How? 3—Do you think Virginia was right or wrong in making up her mind to pay more attention to her marching? Why?

### 28. The Unseen Spectator

Mrs. Phelan was just putting the last sheet on the line when she heard the voice of Father Quinn coming up the concrete walk at the side of the house.

"Mrs. Phelan," said he, "I'm just looking for Bridget. I have here a gold cross on a chain I want to give her. I was watching from the window the ranks leave school today, but none of the children saw me. Some of them just slouched along, scraping their feet, hunchbacked, pushing those beside them, walking on the heels of those in front of them. But Bridget was none of these. She walked like a soldier, head erect, in step, keeping the right distance from those beside her and in front of her. So I am going to give her this present."

You see children, people are watching you when you do not know it; so march in rank like soldiers.

*Questions:* 1—Would you like Father Quinn's present because it was gold or because it was a cross? Why? 2—Would you like somebody to say about you what Father Quinn had to say about the poor marchers? 3—How can you keep him from doing it?

## 29. Young Soldiers

William Tierney and Charles Gaynor did not miss the meaning of the stories about the toy soldiers, the Holy Name procession, and Bridget Phelan's marching. They knew that when little children do not march well they look just as the toy soldiers did after Ruth Jones had arranged them poorly. They were sure that if they wanted their class to look well in leaving school, they would all have to march like Virginia Bell's father in the Holy Name procession. So they made up their minds that they were going to march with heads erect, keeping even distances from the children ahead of them, behind them, and beside them, lifting their feet, and keeping step with the other children. They knew that would make Sister Clara proud, and they wanted to do that very much.

*Questions:* 1—How does one march well? 2—Do you know anybody who marches well? 3—Why ought you to march well leaving school?

## IV. THE AUTHORITY OF THE TEACHER

### 30. The Complaining Lamb

You know that the man who takes care of sheep and lambs is called a shepherd. He takes them to the brook to get nice cool drinks, he guards them from the wolf. But he also watches that they do not run away because if they should run away they might fall into pits, or be chewed up by wild animals. There was once a little lamb, however, who did not like the idea of being guarded so carefully. He complained to his mother of the strictness of the shepherd.

"Why, you silly little woolly lamb," said his mother. "Don't you know the shepherd is so strict just because he loves you, and does not want you to be hurt. He would die rather than let you get hurt."

I do not know whether the lamb quit complaining but I hope he did.

*Questions:* 1—Does the shepherd remind you of anyone you know? 2—Was the complaining lamb like naughty children? Why? 3—Why are shepherds strict with lambs?

### 31. Billy's Complaint

Billy Brady was a little boy of seven. He had just begun school, and thought he could talk as much there as on the street. He never thought about how Our Lord, by not crying, helped St. Joseph to save Him. So one day he complained to Martin Toole, a little boy in his room, just about as old as he.

"O Billy!" said Martin, "are you complaining about Sister telling you to keep quiet. Don't you know you are just like the lamb Sister told us about. You know Sister wants you to keep quiet because she loves you and wants you to listen to what she is telling you."

Billy stopped to think and he felt sure that Martin was right. Sister Beatrice was surprised after that to find how quiet Billy was every day.

*Questions:* 1—Was Billy Brady like Jane Gray? How? 2—Did he forget the story of Our Lord's escape to Egypt? How? 3—Why was Billy like the complaining lamb?

### 32. The Hidden Teacher

Frederick Meyer had just heard Sister say that if he wanted to learn anything in school he would have to keep very quiet. That made him think, and think, and think.

Finally, he said to himself, "Church must be a school; because mother says I must be quiet there. When I go home I am going to ask mother if Church is a school."

So as soon as he went home he asked mother. "Am I supposed to keep quiet in Church because it is a school?"

His mother paused a moment before answering.

Then she said, "Yes, Freddie, everybody in church is there to learn. The Teacher is God, Our Lord, who is behind the gold door you see in the altar. He does not talk like Sister does in school. He only whispers, but if you are still and quiet, you can hear Him plainly."

*Questions:* 1—Why must you keep quiet in school? 2—Why must you keep quiet in church? 3—Who is the Teacher in church? And where is He?

## 33. The Argument

"My teacher knows everything," said Walter Sharp to his friend, Joseph Brown.

"I guess she's not any better than my Sister. She knows everything, too."

"But my Sister helps a fellow lots."

"Say, I suppose you think mine doesn't. Why she even holds my hand steady so I can make those awful r's, and so the k's won't run all over the paper."

"But when you want to know anything, all you have to do is put up your hand and our Sister answers it. I tell you she's smart, she is."

"Same way with our Sister. I tried her out the other day. I asked her when I was born. All she had to do was say how far off is your birthday. I told her six days and she gave me the exact date of my birthday."

The boys were still arguing when I left. I know that each loved his teacher just as you do.

*Questions:* 1—Do you think Walter and Joseph loved their teachers? 2—How can you show your teacher that you love her? 3—Can your teacher do anything that Walter's and Joseph's teacher could not do?

### 34. One Who Knows Everything

"Walter," said Sister Beatrice, "I heard that you told Joseph Brown that I know everything. Did you?"

Walter arose from his seat and said, "Well, don't you?"

Sister said to him, "No, Walter, I do not. I know much more than you. I know many things that I am going to tell you about. But I do not know everything. There is One, however, who does know everything. That is God. He knows everything that ever happened, or ever will happen. He knows what I am saying and what you are thinking. There is nothing He does not know."

*Questions:* 1—Does any man or woman know everything? 2—Who does know everything? 3—What does it mean to know everything? 4—Do you think One who knows everything is a good Teacher?

### 35. William Reed's Resolution

"Oh my!" said William Reed, as Sister Beatrice's class was leaving school for the day. "Did you hear what Sister Beatrice said? She said God knows everything. I feel ashamed. He knows all the bad things I've done."

"Does He even know the bad things you do?" asked Michael Dunn.

"Why sure! Didn't you hear Sister say that there is nothing He does not know. I tell you I'm not going to do anything bad any more."

"Nor I," said Michael, "I don't want to force God to watch me committing sin."

And, dear children, both William and Michael were such good boys after that, their mothers could not explain what had happened to them. I hope you are going to be like them.

*Questions:* 1—Why do people hate to be caught doing wrong? 2—Who always catches everybody when wrong is done? 3—How do you think God feels when He sees people disobeying Him?

### 36. A Large Class-Room

James Kiernan, after hearing the last six stories, said to himself that the whole world is just one big class-room and that the things God asks us to do, He asks us so He can teach us. He decided that he would not complain against God's wishes because he would become worse than the complaining lamb and Billy Brady, if he did. He was sure that while God is in church waiting to teach us, He is everywhere; and that since He knows everything, He can teach us many, many things, if we only do what He tells us. If we refuse to do what He tells us, thought James, we shall miss learning the wonderful things He has to teach.

*Questions:* 1—Why should we want God to teach us? 2—What do we have to do if we want Him to do so? 3—What can we learn from God?

## V. PRAYER

### 37. The Foolish Bear

Once upon a time there was a little bear who was looking for a home, a nice cave in the side of a hill where he could keep warm, and where he would be safe from the wolves. He hunted day after day, hiding himself carefully at night by covering himself up with leaves. One day on his journey he saw a wolf coming towards him, and he started to run. But the wolf called and told him not to run away, that he would not hurt him. The silly bear believed the wolf and waited for him.

"What are you doing?" asked the wolf.

"I'm looking for a home," said the bear.

"Oh! you don't need a home, come and live with me."

"But you might eat me up," said the bear. "My mother told me that wolves eat little bears."

"Oh! don't believe your mother. She just doesn't like wolves, that's all. Why I never knew of a wolf eating a bear. Won't you come to my house to stay?"

The poor bear said he would. The bear and wolf talked all the way to the wolf's home. When bed-time came, the wolf told the bear to go to bed. But the little bear became afraid and would not go. Then the wolf became very angry, and decided to eat the bear right away. He took one bite, but the bear got away and ran as fast as he could. He kept away from wolves after that.

*Questions:* 1—What was the little bear's first and greatest mistake? 2—If you had been the little bear, would you have trusted the wolf? 3—Which do you think should have been believed, the bear's mother or the nasty wolf?

N. B.—For teachers' helps see page 183.

## 38. The Devil's Lies

Father Walsh came in to the first grade one day and asked the children if they ever heard the story of the foolish bear. All the boys and girls said they had.

"Well," said Father Walsh, "did you ever stop to think that the devil is like that wolf? He sees a little boy or girl hunting for a home in heaven by being good. He invites that little boy or girl to go with him. He says that he wouldn't hurt any little boy or girl, and that whoever said he would told an awful lie. Then when the foolish boy and girl listens to him, he takes hold of them all of a sudden and drags them down to his home in hell where they will burn forever."

*Questions:* 1—What home are boys and girls hunting? 2—Who is the wolf? Why do you say so? 3—Will you let the wolf keep you from your home?

## 39. The Greedy Mouse

Two little brother mice named Teeny and Tiny left their country home to go to the city. Before they left, mother gave them strict orders not to be greedy. Soon after they came to the city a party was held in the house where they made their home. Tiny invited himself to the party but Teeny warned him of what their mother had told them. It was a party of little boys and girls, and of course, there were lots of cakes. Tiny ran under the table and was having a good time eating cake crumbs while Teeny was out in the kitchen with nothing but bread crumbs to eat. All of a sudden one of the little girls saw Tiny and screamed. Tiny tried to get out but just as he was passing through the doorway, the little girl's father hit him on the back with a stick.

He could hardly walk after that.  Teeny saw it all from a corner of the kitchen.

"Oh! if you had not been so greedy," said he, "you would not have been hurt."

*Questions:* 1—Was the mother of the mice just trying to make it hard for them when she told them not to be greedy? 2—Would you like to be like Teeny or Tiny?  Why?  3—Will greedy boys and girls be punished?  How?

N. B.—For teachers' helps see page 187.

### 40. Danny's Lesson

Danny Shea's mother had bought a whole lot of cooking apples, intending to make apple butter with them.  As soon as Danny came home he saw the apples and immediately commenced to coax his mother to give him some.  She did not want to do this because she was afraid the apples might hurt him.  She told him this, but he pouted.  As soon as mother's back was turned he took three and ate them.  About an hour after he threw himself on the couch crying with pain. The apples had given him cramps.

Mother knew what was wrong with him, but she simply said, "I guess I won't let you die this time."

Soon the doctor had come.  After he had cared for Danny, he warned him to listen to his mother, but not to the devil in the future.

*Questions:* 1—How was Danny's mother like the mother of the mice?  2—How was Danny like Tiny?  3—Did Danny's mother love him?  Why?

### 41. Give Us Our Daily Bread

Our Lord told us to say in the prayer that He made up for us Himself and which we call the Lord's Prayer, "Give us this day our daily bread."  I suppose that many of you know how to say that prayer by this time. Well, when Our Lord told us to say that He meant that we should ask for the things we need to be good. Of course, we need to eat. But He wants us to ask also for the things that will make us holy, for power to pray often, to fool the devil, to keep away from sin. How many of you do that?

*Questions:* 1—Are we greedy if we ask God for what we need? 2—What kind of things ought we to ask God for? 3—What should we be most anxious to get from Him?

## 42. The Unanswered Prayer

A little girl, named Martha Ryan, told the priest at her parish church that she had prayed, and prayed, very, very hard for a new baby doll for Christmas, and she had not been answered.

"Well, you had one baby doll, hadn't you?" asked Father Meyer.

"Oh, yes! but that is not enough!"

The reason her prayer was not answered was, as Father Meyer showed her, because she was greedy. He warned her that if she kept on being so greedy the same thing would happen to her that happened to the mouse and to Danny Shea. I am sure that none of the little boys and girls here want such a thing to happen to them.

*Questions:* 1—Can we be greedy in asking God for things? How? 2—Do the prayers of the greedy get an answer? Why? 3—Why wasn't Martha Ryan's prayer answered?

## 43. Dangerous Gifts

Vincent Snyder heard the story of Martha Ryan's prayer. He remembered that he had asked for some things that he never had.  His parents were poor and he hardly ever got any toys for Christmas.  He prayed, and prayed for them, but no toys ever came.  So he asked Father Burke why his prayer wasn't answered. Father Burke told him that when God sees that certain things are not good for us He will not give them, because He wants to save us from Hell.

"Would your mother allow your little brother, Bill, to play with the butcher-knife?" he asked.

Vincent said, "No, certainly not; she'd be afraid he'd cut himself."

"But Bill sometimes cries for the knife, doesn't he?"

"He sure does," Vincent admitted.

"Well sometimes we cry to God for things that are just as dangerous as knives.  God will not give them to us because He doesn't want us to cut ourselves."

*Questions:* 1—Give some reasons why our prayers are not answered.  2—Would you like God to give you something that would make you lose your soul?  3—Do you always know what is good, and what is bad for you?

## 44. Impoliteness Towards God

Raymond Beck put up his hand as soon as he had heard what Vincent Snyder said and asked Father Burke, "Sometimes people do not get what they ask for because they don't pay any attention to God when they are asking for it, isn't that so, Father?"

Father Burke was pleased.

"Yes, that's right.  Suppose, for instance, that you wanted Sister to excuse you from the room.  When you came up to ask her, instead of looking as though you meant what you said, you looked out of the window. Do you think you would get what you ask her for?"

The children all said they thought not.

"Well," said Father Burke, "when some children pray they never even think of God, they are impolite to Him. No wonder they do not get what they ask for."

*Questions:* 1—When you want people to listen to what you say, how do you talk to them? 2—How do some people talk to God when they think about dollies, and games, and other things like that? 3—Would you give a person who was impolite what he asked for?

### 45. Reasons for Prayer

Francis McGuirk said to his mother that just because the devil tries to fool us as the wolf fooled the little bear, we ought to be careful to pray always. Otherwise he was sure we would commit sins of many kinds through being selfish.

Mother was surprised to find that Francis knew the devil fights us by trying to make us think he is giving us good things for ourselves.

"But," said Francis, "the things he gives only hurt us like the green apples hurt Danny Shea. Sometimes, they might even make us lose our souls, as the cake crumbs caused Tiny to be hurt. When I pray I am going to remember not to be greedy as Danny and the mouse were."

"What do you mean, Francis?" asked his mother.

"Why I mean I am not going to ask for the things I don't need. And even when I ask for things I do need, I'm not going to be disappointed if I don't get them."

"That's right," said his mother. "Maybe God sees that they will hurt you."

"And above all, when I talk to God, I am going to

pray as though I meant what I said, paying strict attention to everything."

Mrs. McGuirk was very much pleased to find that Francis had learned so much about prayer in the short time he had been at school.

*Questions:* 1—Does the devil like to give us good things or bad? 2—Does he like to fool us? 3—What are you going to pray for when you talk to God? 4—How will you talk to Him? 5—Will you be disappointed if you don't get what you asked for?

## VI. THE LORD'S PRAYER

### 46. The Black Chick

Once upon a time there was a beautiful white hen who had nine white chicks and one black one. She loved all her chicks, the black one as well as the white ones. But the white chicks did not love the black one. They would not play with it. They called it names, and tried to hurt it. This made the mother hen sad, and she took the little black chick under her wing to keep it safe. She told the others that they should love the black chick because it was their brother. God is the father of all of us. He loves His black children as well as His white children. He wants His black children and His white children to love each other.

*Questions:* 1—Why did the mother hen love the black chick as well as the white chicks? 2—Do you think the white chicks were sorry for what they did? 3—Why should black children and white children love each other?

N. B.—For teachers' helps see page 191.

### 47. Our Black Brethren

Sister Mary Clarence told the story of the little black chick to her class one day and then added that the boys and girls there must not treat black people badly.

"They are our brothers and sisters," she said.

Little Danny Dugan could not understand that so he said, "How can black people be related to white?"

"Why," said Sister, "we have all the same Father. God is the Father of all of us. How do you commence the Lord's Prayer?" she asked.

Danny shuffled around for a moment because he didn't know exactly what she meant by the Lord's Prayer.

"Of course you know," said Sister. "It's that prayer we say first in the morning."

"Oh! you mean the 'Our Father?'" asked Danny.

"Yes," said Sister, "you say, 'Our Father,' don't you? Not, 'My Father,' but 'Our Father,' because He is the Father of all of us."

*Questions:* 1—Do we have any brothers and sisters besides the ones at home? 2—Who is the Father of all of us? 3—How and when do we remind ourselves of that?

## 48. The Fox and His Home

A fox once started out into the world to make a home for himself. Before leaving his mother she told him that until he found a home, he should be careful to hide himself at night so that the wolf would not catch him, and make a meal of him. For a good many days the fox obeyed his mother, but finally getting tired of looking for a home, he lay down one night in the open, by the side of the road along which he was traveling. That fox never awoke. The wolf killed him and ate him. Will you be disobedient and neglect your mother's instruction as this fox did?

*Questions:* 1—What is the difference between the fox and the foolish little bear? 2—What was the mistake of the fox? 3—Show how the bear and fox were disobedient in different ways.

### 49. Clara Boyle Seeks a Home

Sister Irene told the story of the fox and the home he was seeking, but never found, to her class of little children.

She had scarcely finished it when Clara Boyle put up her hand and said, "But, Sister, I will never get tired looking for my home."

All the little children looked surprised. They never thought that Clara was an orphan. They thought she had a very good home. She soon explained. She told them that she had a very good home here on earth, but that she would have to leave it some day. Her hope was to go to a home she would never lose, to her home in heaven.

*Questions:* 1—Why do you think that Clara Boyle heard the story of how the devil is like a wolf keeping us from home? 2—Do you think the other children who were surprised at what she said had heard that story? Why? 3—Which home, the one here or heaven, will make you happier?

### 50. A Lesson from the Fox

On her way home from school Clara repeated what she had told Sister to Frances Carney, her playmate.

"No, indeed, I never will let the old wolf get me."

"What wolf do you mean, Clara? I don't think there are any wolves around here. I know if I thought there were I would run, and run faster than Little Red Riding Hood ever could run."

"Well, I hope you do run that fast when the wolf I mean comes around; I mean the devil. You know he is just as anxious to get your soul as the wolf was to chew up the fox."

"Indeed, I never allow him to get near me," answered Frances.

"And don't go to sleep either, without saying your night prayers and covering yourself up with those prayers, because if you do, the devil may be watching his chance to catch you. If you pray at night before going to bed, he'll never see you."

*Questions:* 1—Why do you think the stories of the foolish bear and the fox helped Clara to be good? 2—Why do you think Frances was a good little girl, too? 3—What are the leaves you have to cover yourself with at night?

### 51. The Most Beautiful Home

Somehow or other Clara Boyle could not forget about that story of the fox. When daddy came home from work that night she climbed up on his knee and told him all about it.

"But I am going to keep on looking for my home," said she.

"Why, haven't you a fine home here? Just look at this beautiful furniture, and those fine curtains, and this lovely carpet. And there is your nursery. What toy is there made that you don't have?"

"Oh! I know this home is beautiful, but it is not nearly so beautiful as my home in heaven, because there I shall have not only you and mamma, but also One whom I love much more. You know we say in the Lord's Prayer, 'Our Father, who art in heaven,' don't we? Well it's God's home; and if I get there God and I shall live together in the same home."

*Questions:* 1—Why do you think Clara did right in telling her daddy the story of the fox? 2—Do you think that Clara's daddy was jealous when she told him that she loved God more than him? 3—When do we remind ourselves of our Father's and our most beautiful home?

## 52. Denis, the Champion

"Here, here, Denis, haven't I told you not to fight? Let that boy alone. I know he's bigger than you are, but if you punch him once more, I'll make you stay in tomorrow for an hour."

It was Father Flynn's voice. Denis was surely sorry to be caught fighting. He quit right away. The big boy whom he had been fighting with, sneaked away.

"I'm sorry, Father," said Denis. "I know I promised a whole lot of times not to fight any more. But this coward just got me worked up and I couldn't help it."

"Why, what did he do, Denis, to make you so angry?"

Denis blushed. He didn't want to tell Father Flynn. Finally, he decided he had better tell everything.

So he said, "We were talking about how good Father Kennedy is to all of us. That big coward is not a Catholic and when he heard what we were speaking about he curled his lip, spoke Father Kennedy's name, and then spit out afterwards, as though it left a bad taste in his mouth. He hardly had the spit out of his mouth until he had one on the jaw."

"Indeed, I am glad to see you standing up for the priest's name, but you know what the fifth commandment says. That boy may never act the same way before you again. But he doesn't love Father Kennedy any more. There is only one way to help boys who are like him and that is to pray for them. But, Denis, since you obeyed me and quit fighting when I told you, I will let you off if you promise never to fight again."

It didn't take Denis long to make the promise.

*Questions:* 1—What do you like most about Denis? 2—Do you think he respected the priest? Why? 3—Why should he respect the priest's name? 4—Would you try to prove things by fighting?

## 53. A Name to Be Respected

The day after the fight Father Flynn went into Denis McTighe's room and told the story of the fight and its cause without mentioning any names. He said he was proud that the boys respected the name of the priest.

"There is another name that we ought to respect still more. We pray daily that people may honor it and love it. You know that in the 'Our Father,' you say, 'hallowed be Thy name.' That means that you want yourself and others to love the name of God. I hope you do not forget that prayer when you hear others taking God's name in vain. I hope you are just as anxious to have God's name respected as you are to have the priest's."

Many of the boys had never thought of this. They all made up their minds to act as Father Flynn had asked them.

*Questions:* 1—Whose name ought to be respected more than the priest's? 2—How do people show disrespect to that name? 3—When do we remind ourselves that we want ourselves and everybody to show it the proper respect?

## 54. Child Preachers

"O boy! maybe I wouldn't like to be able to preach like Father Gallagher," said Joseph Harrison to

Theodore Johnson one day as they were playing marbles in the school yard. "You can talk about being great, but all I would like to do would be to get up there in the pulpit and say those swell things that he says; to make people sad and make them happy just by the way I would say them."

Sister Constance overheard what Joseph said.

"You can be a preacher right now, if you want to be," said she.

Joseph thought she was teasing him and he blushed.

"That's true," she added; "if you live a good life, that is, obey, be honest and truthful, respect God's name and the like, you will be showing others how to do the same thing."

*Questions:* 1—Tell me what priest you like to hear preaching and why. 2—Why does the priest preach? 3—How can little children preach?

## 55. Young Apostles

Sister Constance repeated to her class that afternoon what she had heard one of the boys (she did not mention his name) say in the school yard. She told them that if they were good and obedient boys and girls they would make people Catholics.

"You know," she said, "they will see how good you are and they will wonder what is making you so good. Then someone will say that you are a Catholic. That will make them think well of the Catholic Church. Soon they will ask about it, and finally they may become Catholics just because of your goodness. If you are good, therefore, you can help the Church to grow."

*Questions:* 1—Would you like some non-Catholics to have the good things you have in the Catholic Church? 2—Does

God want them all to have them? 3—Can you help God to make them Catholics? How?

## 56. A Prayer for Growth

"I know that you all want the Church to grow," said Father Gallagher, who came in just as Sister Constance was telling them how to make people Catholic. "If you don't, I can't understand why you are always praying for it. Every time you say the 'Our Father,' you say, 'Thy kingdom come.' When you say that, you are asking God to make His kingdom, which is the Church, come to more and more people; you are asking God to make His Church grow. Do not forget that prayer when you have a chance to work with God. It's not enough to pray. God many times makes converts through us men and women, and more often through little children. Show the people how good the Catholic Church can make you, and the Catholic Church will grow, and your prayer will be answered."

*Questions:* 1—Do you think that God can make you better preachers? 2—Do you think you ought to ask Him to make you such? 3—When do all Catholics ask God that they may give good example?

## 57. Why May Loved the Squirrels

"Well, what in the world are you doing, you dear fuzzy squirrel?" asked May one September afternoon as she walked through the woods and saw a dear little squirrel with a big, bushy tail gathering nuts for the winter. Now if you heard a squirrel talk I'm sure you would be astonished. Indeed, May Byrne was astonished when she heard the squirrel say that he was doing what God wanted him to do. She never thought that squirrels obey God, but they do and I can vouch for the squirrel's word.   Every bit of it is true.

*Questions:* 1—Does a squirrel think like you and I?   2—How does the squirrel know that it ought to gather nuts for winter?   3—Does the squirrel give boys and girls a good example?

N. B.—For teachers' helps see page 195.

### 58. Caroline's Sermon

"Now, don't be giving me any of your sermons, Caroline.  You're not a priest."  This was what Gertrude Rannegan said to Caroline Fitzpatrick, who was trying to show her how the squirrel is better than some children who will not do what God wants.

"That's just the trouble with us children," continued Caroline.   "We think that everything good that's told us is nothing but a sermon.   Now you know as well as I do that God wants us to be obedient to our parents and superiors.   You also know how often we will not do what God wants.   If that is not allowing a squirrel to love God more than we do, I must say that I don't know what is."

I agree with Caroline.   Don't you?

*Questions:* 1—Do people have to be priests to give sermons, to preach?  2—What was wrong, then, with what Gertrude Rannegan said to Caroline Fitzpatrick?  3—Why was Caroline's sermon a good one?

### 59. Father Brown's Gift

"Yes," said Caroline Fitzpatrick to her mother, "Father Brown gave me this beautiful rosary after he heard me telling a little girl friend that the squirrel is better than we are because it obeys God.   Then Father

Brown said that what he could never understand was why people prayed that everybody might do what God wants, and then refuse to do it themselves. He proved that we all pray for people to do what God wants. You know we say in the 'Our Father,' 'Thy Will be done on earth as it is in Heaven.' Now, mother, you know that means we wish that everybody would do just what God wants, the same as all the angels and saints do in Heaven."

I wish you would have seen Mrs. Fitzpatrick's face when Caroline was through speaking. My! but she was pleased. And I wouldn't mind having the fine dish of ice cream that Caroline got that night for knowing so much about the "Our Father."

*Questions:* 1—Was the rosary the only reward Caroline got for giving that good sermon? Do you think God gave her a reward? 2—When do we pray that we may follow the example of the squirrel? 3—Do you think that people are fools to say they want something and then show they don't want it by what they do? 4—How do boys and girls show themselves foolish?

N. B.—The sixth clause of the Lord's Prayer, "Give us this day our daily bread," has already been treated. See Story No. 41.

## 60. The Pout

"She had no business treating me mean. I'll never talk to her again." Florence Golden's mother heard her say this about a little girl friend who had laughed when she made a mistake in spelling a word.

"Well," said her mother, "the little girl had no right to laugh, but still don't you remember the story the crucifix tells us? God died on the Cross. While He was dying some bad men laughed and laughed at Him.

Did He get angry? No, Florence, He prayed for them. You must, at least, make up with your little girl friend."

*Questions:* 1—Why don't you like a pout? 2—Did anybody laugh at Our Lord? Did He get angry? 3—What must be done to follow Our Lord's example in this matter?

### 61. The Cross of Forgiveness

After Mrs. Golden had finished talking Mr. Golden said to Florence. "I guess you forget that when Our Lord died on the Cross He forgave you for all the times you talked in church. If that is not insulting Our Lord, who is right there in church, then nothing is. But Our Lord does not hold spite. Are you going to turn your back on Our Lord, and after He has forgiven you refuse to forgive a little girl, who has merely laughed a little because you said something that sounded funny?"

Florence commenced to cry and said she was sorry she had pouted, and would not do it again.

*Questions:* 1—Do naughty children sometimes offend Our Lord? How? 2—Does He pout? How do you know? 3—What hard thing did He do for those who hurt Him?

### 62. The Two Debts

Did you ever know Our Lord told stories to the people when He was teaching them? Well He did. One time He told them a story about two men whom we will call Frank and James. Now Frank and James both worked for a man named Mr. Smith. Frank owed Mr. Smith a thousand dollars, and James owed Frank a hundred dollars. When the time to pay came, Mr. Smith was going to put Frank in jail for not paying, but Frank begged him so hard that he decided to wait.

Then Frank met James and said, "Where's my money?"

James couldn't pay, so Frank had him arrested. When Mr. Smith heard this he had Frank arrested. He was very sorry to learn that after he promised Frank to wait for a thousand dollars, Frank would not wait for the hundred that James owed him.

*Questions:* 1—Is it easier to wait for the payment of a debt of a thousand dollars, or of a hundred? 2—Would you rather be like Mr. Smith or like Frank? 3—Do you think that Frank got what he deserved? Why?

### 63. William Herron's Debt

William Herron heard the story about the two debts, and he thought it over and over in his mind. The same afternoon he said to Sister Mary Ida.

"You know, Sister Mary Ida, I think I am like Frank, and that God is like Mr. Smith. God forgives me many things, but I think that He must want me to forgive my friends who have not hurt me nearly so much as I have hurt God."

Sister Mary Ida was very glad to see that William knew Our Lord's meaning.

She said to him, "You know that you ask God to forgive you just the same as you forgive those who have hurt you. You say in the 'Our Father,' 'Forgive us our trespasses as we forgive those who trespass against us.' Now, if you don't forgive those who hurt you, you tell God not to forgive you, either."

I feel sure that every boy and girl here is going to remember this and forgive those who have hurt him or her.

*Questions:* 1—Do we hurt God more than other children hurt us? 2—Does He forgive us when we hurt Him? 3—Ought we to forgive others who hurt us? 4—When do we ask God to forgive us just as we forgive others?

### 64. The Little Puppy

There was once a little puppy whose mother always warned it against running after moving things like bicycles and autos. She told him he would surely be hurt if he did. One day the puppy saw a motorcycle coming. It made a great deal of noise. The puppy had never seen one before, so he thought he would be very brave, and run after it. He thought he was too big to have to mind his mother. But the motorcycle hit him and hurt his leg, and he limped back to his mother. After that he was always careful to do as his mother told him.

*Questions:* 1—Is it safe to be disobedient? 2—Was the puppy really as big and brave as he thought he was? 3—What makes us forget the danger of sin? Who makes us forget?

N. B.—For teachers' helps see page 198.

### 65. The Mouse and the Match

There was once a mother mouse who lived under a kitchen. She taught all the little mice not to play with matches because matches are dangerous, and may burn people up. One day one of the mice crawled up into the kitchen and saw some matches on the floor. At first he remembered what his mother had told him and instead of going to eat the matches he ran all around the floor looking for crumbs. Shortly the mouse thought he would like to eat one of the matches. At first, he just licked. Then he bit it. As he did so, it lighted, and the mouse was burned very badly. He told his mother how sorry he was for not doing as she told him.

*Questions:* 1—Did the mouse eat the match as soon as he saw it? 2—What was the cause of his eating it? 3—What should children do when temptation comes to them? Should they play with it, or run away quickly from it?

N. B.—For teachers' helps see page 201.

### 66. Genevieve's Comparison

Genevieve Harper was a very bright pupil and so when Sister M. Frederick had told her class the stories of the little puppy and the disobedient mouse, she thought to herself:

"Now isn't that just the way we would act if we listened to the devil? He would like to make us think we are brave and big, or that matches are good to eat. If he can fool us, he will make us commit sin, which hurts our souls just as the puppy and mouse were hurt. Indeed, I am not going to allow the devil to fool me."

*Questions:* 1—How does the devil fool us? 2—Does he ever tell us that sin is bad for us? 3—Would we commit sin, if he did?

### 67. Genevieve Meets Her Equal

Genevieve told Martha Fox of the things she had been turning over in her mind after she heard the stories of the puppy and the mouse. She spoke about how the devil tries to get hold of our souls by coaxing us to show off.

"Why, Genevieve Harper," said Martha, "you talk as though you were the only one who thought about how the devil tempts us when those stories were told. I was thinking of it, too. And while I was thinking about it, it seemed to me that the devil makes us think he is anxious to give us a fine piece of candy with a strawberry center. If we are foolish enough to take it, we shall find not a strawberry center, but mud in the middle of it."

"That was a good thought," said Genevieve, "I am not going to be angry with you about it, because I am glad to see the devil caught. I wish every girl and boy in our class thought about how to fool the devil, just as you and I did."

*Questions:* 1—Are things always as good as they seem? 2—Whom should you believe to find out whether things are really good? 3—What is the mud under the chocolate spoken of by Martha Fox?

### 68. Help Against Satan

Sister Frederick must have been thinking about the devil and his temptations, too, because the next day she told the children of her class that the same thing that happened to the puppy and the mouse would happen to them if they did not chase the devil away from them. Genevieve and Martha both smiled for they had thought about the same thing even before Sister told them about it.

"But," added Sister, "there is no reason for such a thing happening to any of you. God promised to give us what we pray for, if it is good for us. Now in the 'Our Father' you say, 'Lead us not into temptation.' By that prayer you are begging God for help to chase away the devil when he tempts you. And God gives you the help you need. Don't forget to use it."

*Questions:* 1—Do you think you could tell whether or not the devil is trying to fool you if God didn't help you? 2—

Does God know whether the candy is real or only mud? 3—
Tell me what you say when you ask Our Lord in the Lord's
Prayer to tell you what is really good, and what is not?

## 69. Pain and Prayer

"Oh! my toothache is no better. And I've prayed
hard, and hard, and hard. Still it pains just as much
as before." This was what George Greb was saying to
his companions when Father Flanagan came up.

"Why, George," he said, "don't you know that pains
are sometimes good things? Pains make us think of
what Christ, Our Lord, suffered on the Cross for us
and so help us to keep away from sin. God sometimes
refuses to take pains away because He knows that they
are going to make people better and keep them away
from sin. So keep on praying, George. But if the
toothache does not stop just say to yourself that God
is allowing it to stay to make you a better boy."

*Questions:* 1—Does God sometimes allow us to suffer?
What for? 2—Will He always take pain away from us if we
pray? 3—Did He show us how to suffer?

## 70. Holding a Job

George told Sister Helen what Father Flanagan had
said to him, because he thought he might get sympathy.

Instead Sister said to him, "George, you sell papers,
don't you? Well, suppose you got a real, good corner,
where lots of people passed, and where you sold lots
of papers, would you like to give up that corner for a
poorer one? I know you wouldn't. Still, you have to
work harder there. If you had an easier corner you
might have time to play marbles even, but you wouldn't
make much money, would you? Well the people who

don't have pains, have the easy corners, they are not working very hard for God, and when pay-day comes they won't get much money. So you ought to thank God for your pains because He gives you the good corners where you will earn the most for heaven."

*Questions:* 1—Who makes the more money, the one who works hard or the one who works very little? 2—Who makes the most for pay-day in heaven? 3—Is bearing pain one way of working for pay in heaven?

## 71. A Reward for Sacrifice

Virginia Padden was practising for the May procession and had been given the very first place in line. She was very proud of that. She kept thinking of how nice she would look and what the people would say about her. But about two weeks before the procession, she had a bad cold and the doctor made her stay home for a week. She worried about giving up that fine place in the procession. But daddy told her about Our Lord leaving His fine place in heaven just to come and save us. When Virginia went back to school she told Sister she was going to be like Our Lord; she would take any place that was left. The only place left was that of Queen of May. The little girl who was to be that was sick. So Virginia got that place, the best of all, as a reward for being unselfish.

*Questions:* 1—Would you want to march in a procession just to show off? 2—Why do you think Virginia had a good daddy? 3—How did Virginia deserve her reward?

## 72. Dorothy's Roses

Long years ago the Catholics had to have Mass down in tunnels because bad men wanted to kill them. One time some of these Catholics were arrested, and one of them was a young girl named Dorothy. The men coaxed her to quit being a Catholic but she paid no attention to them. They said they would kill her. She said she would get to heaven that much sooner. They laughed at her. She told them that when she got to heaven she would send them a sign to show that she was there.

A few moments after she had been killed a little boy with a basket of roses came up to the soldiers and said, "Dorothy sends you these from heaven."

Then the boy suddenly went out of sight. The soldier that had been meanest to Dorothy was converted by this and became a Christian.

*Questions:* 1—Was it harder to be a Catholic long years ago than it is now? 2—How do you know that Dorothy loved Our Lord? 3—What are you willing to do to show Our Lord you love Him?

N. B.—For teachers' helps see page 205.

### 73. The Resolution of Frances McGreevey

When Frances McGreevey heard how brave Dorothy had been, even though the soldiers laughed at her, and when she saw how Dorothy was rewarded, she felt ashamed of herself for having been so impatient when she was sick. She told her mother on arriving home from school that night what Dorothy had done. Her mother had never heard the story before and listened very attentively.

"She was a brave girl, wasn't she?" asked her mother.

"Yes, and I'm going to be like her," said Frances.

"We don't want our Frances to die yet."

"Oh! I won't have to die; men don't often kill people for their religion any more. But I'm going to be more brave while I live, and suffer patiently like Dorothy."

*Questions:* 1—Were you ever impatient like Frances? 2—Did the story of Dorothy's death help Frances? How? 3—When is it hard to be patient for Our Lord?

### 74. "Deliver Us from Evil"

"Now, boys and girls," said Father Cavanaugh, "none of us likes to suffer. Sometimes we have to do it. Then if we are patient, God loves us. Still, we want to keep pains and aches, and scoldings, and whippings as far away from us as we can. So when we say the 'Our Father' we ask God to keep them away from us when we say, 'Deliver us from evil.' "

"But," asked Lillian Thompson, "you didn't mention anything about sin. You said we all want to keep far away from pains and aches and troubles, but what about sin? Isn't that worse than all other evils?"

"Indeed yes," answered the priest, "and that's the reason we ask God to save us from it before we ask for safety from other evils. You know in the 'Our Father' we say first, 'Lead us not into temptation,' that is, 'keep us out of sin,' and then, 'but deliver us from evil.' Indeed, I am pleased to see such a bright little girl in class, and I want you all to remember what she said, and to steer away from sin because it surely is the worst thing that can happen. To be disobedient just once is worse than having a toothache a hundred times."

The boys and girls all said they would remember the lesson Father had given them.

*Questions:* 1—Does God want us to suffer sometimes? 2—Is it all right to pray that we won't have to suffer? 3—When do you ask God to keep you from suffering?

## 75. A Prayer to the Father

"My! didn't we learn a whole lot about the 'Our Father'?" asked Michael Thompson of Gilbert Shay, his friend.

"Yes, we learned that God is our Father, the Father of all of us."

"And that His home is heaven where we all must try to go."

"Don't forget," warned Gilbert, "that in the 'Our Father' we pray that God's name may be honored by everybody."

"I won't" answered Michael, "and I hope you are trying to make the prayer, 'Thy kingdom come' have an answer by showing good example to non-Catholics."

"I am trying hard to do it. But are you doing God's will in everything? You know you ask in the 'Our Father' that everybody may do God's will here as the angels do it in Heaven."

"Yes, I try hard to do what God wants. And I never forget to ask Him for my daily bread, or food for my body and soul. Besides that, I always try hard to forgive other people when they hurt me, because I know that in the 'Our Father' I ask God to forgive me."

"And I," concluded Gilbert, "always ask God very earnestly to save me from the temptation of the devil and from other evils. Pain, sickness, and trouble I don't mind if God wants me to have them. Of course, I'd rather not have them. But sin and the devil are two things I always want to be very far away from."

"Same here," concluded Michael.

I think these boys knew a great deal about the "Our Father," don't you?

*Questions:* 1—What have you learned from the stories about the "Our Father"? 2—What two things do we ask to be saved from in the "Our Father"? 3—What do we ask for when we say, "Give us this day our daily bread"?

## VII. THE HAIL MARY

### 76. Proud Jean

There was once a bright little girl named Jean O'Brien who always knew her lessons except one day when thè school visitor came to visit the school, and it seemed then that she knew not a thing. She went home bitterly disappointed, but in a dream she had that night she thought Our Lord came to her, and patted her head, and told her why she had been allowed to make the mistake, because she was getting too proud, and had forgotten to ask Him for help.

"I love you," He said, "and the less you think of yourself, and the less you show off the more I will love you."

Do you think Jean was proud after that? Well, I know she was not. She worked still harder at her lessons, but always asked Him to help her.

*Questions:* 1—How does the devil tempt children that are bright? 2—How did Our Lord save Jean from committing sin? 3—Are you going to be like Jean before or after the dream? Why?

N. B.—For teachers' helps see page 210.

### 77. An Awful Fall

Before God made the first man and woman He made some people that do not have any bodies at all. They have no eyes, no ears, no hands, no feet, they have

nothing that belongs to the body. They are all soul.
Now, you know that you can not see your soul with
your eyes. But you can feel it. If you were dead,
you could not move your hand, because the soul would
not be there to work. So you feel the soul, but can
not see it. These people God made, therefore, we can
not see. In the beginning God wanted to make them
earn heaven, just as we have to work for it by being
good. So He gave them a chance to see whether they
were going to be with Him or against Him. Well, one
of them who was very bright, forgot that God had
made him bright, and so he became very proud. He
even thought he was as good as God, and he wanted
to have people think as much of him as God. It wasn't
long until he was a very, very sorry person. My
goodness! but he was chased out of heaven quickly.
Not only that, but he must burn forever, as God's enemy, trying to do everything he can to hurt God. That
person is the devil. I hope that you will remember
the awful fall he had, and not be like him. Be like
Jean. Remember that if you are bright, it is God that
has made you so.

*Questions:* 1—Why can not you see your soul? 2—How
does the story of Jean remind you of that proud person who
forgot that God made him bright? 3—What happened to him
for being proud? What does that teach you?

## 78. Special Messengers

Michael Quinn and Patrick Gallagher were both
messenger boys, who worked after school for a department store, carrying packages to people who had bought
at the store.

"I surely do get tired carrying packages," said

Michael. "I do wish we were not so poor, so I wouldn't have to work."

"Oh!" said Patrick, "do you forget that you are not acting as messenger only for the department store, but also for God. It's God who wants you to be a messenger, so why not be a good one?"

"I know that's what mother tells me. But it's so hard to remember that. I wish God would tell me to go on these errands like He tells the angels. You know, don't you, that that's one of the things the people in heaven whom God created without a body, have to do. God sends them as messengers down here to earth. Well, if God would say to me, as He does to the angels, 'Michael, go to such and such a place,' why I'd run, and run, and run; and I tell you that would be the fastest errand I'd ever be on."

"Well," said Patrick, "when the 'boss' tells you, it's as though God were speaking to you. I always think of that and it makes my work very easy."

Before they had left each other to go on different errands, Patrick had made Michael think the same as he did.

*Questions:* 1—What is one of the things that God wants the people in heaven called angels to do for him? 2—Why do you think Patrick studied harder than Michael? 3—Does God sometimes ask you to go on errands? When?

### 79. On an Errand

When Laura Bauer had heard the story of the two messenger boys she remembered quite clearly the story she had heard of one of heaven's people, whom God created without a body, coming to earth as a messenger from God. Laura thought over in her mind what

God must have said to the angel, for that was what the messenger was, when He sent him here.

She thought God said something like this, "Gabriel (for that was the angel's name), I want you to go down to that sweet young girl you see praying there all alone, and tell her that God is coming down on earth to save all men, and that she has been chosen to be His Mother."

Then Laura pictured how quickly the angel would run on this errand, and she heard him, in her mind, saying to Mary, the sweet young girl who was the Blessed Virgin,

"Hail Mary, full of grace, the Lord is with thee."

Then, of a sudden she remembered that she had the right to say to the Blessed Virgin, the same thing that the angel did.

Every time she said the "Hail Mary" she commenced by saying, "Hail Mary, full of grace, the Lord is with thee."

I tell you that Laura never forgot that when she said the "Hail Mary," after that.

*Questions:* 1—To whom was the angel Gabriel sent? 2—What was his message? 3—When do we say the same words that the angel said?

## 80. Preparing the Way

"You never heard of John the Baptist? And you a Catholic! Why, I'm ashamed of you," said Edward Schaeffer to Henry Trainor. "Why John the Baptist was the man that came to talk to the people, to tell that in a few months Our Lord was coming out to talk to them Himself. He wanted them to get rid of their sins so that they wouldn't be ashamed to stand before Our Lord, who, of course, could have seen every sin on their souls."

"Did many people listen to him?" asked Henry.

"O yes! a good many. You know what great crowds listened to Our Lord, don't you? Well a whole lot of them were prepared for His preaching through the talks of John the Baptist. I hope you don't forget this, and that you'll be able to tell any Protestant or non-Catholic who John the Baptist was, if he asks you."

*Questions:* 1—Who came to get the people ready to see Our Lord? 2—How did he get them ready? 3—Do you know anybody that reminds you of John the Baptist (the priest)?

### 81. Cousins

"How would you like to be a cousin of Our Lord?" asked Loretta Anderson of her little friend, Wilma Gardner, one day after they had been reading together of the wonderful things He did.

"I wouldn't even want that much. All I would want to be would be a special friend of His. Why, if He would even shake hands with me, I know I would never forget it."

"But you would be still happier, wouldn't you," asked Loretta, "if you were His cousin?"

"I'd be so happy I wouldn't know how to keep from laughing or crying with joy."

"Well, Saint John the Baptist was a cousin of Our Lord. I guess he must have been very happy. Don't you think so?"

"Now I know why he was able to preach so well, and make the people get ready for Our Lord. I think if I were Our Lord's cousin, I could do it, too."

I hope, dear children, that you are all trying to be

friends of God, even though you are not His cousins, so that you can preach about Him by your good example.

*Questions:* 1—Would you like to be Our Lord's special friend? 2—Who was His cousin? 3—Do you think being Our Lord's cousin made him preach well?

## 82. Pleasant News

Sister Blandina was teaching her class about the visit of the angel Gabriel to the Blessed Virgin.

"Besides telling her," she said, "that she was going to be God's mother, he also spoke about the man who was going to get the people ready to listen to God when He would start to preach to them. The angel told the Blessed Virgin that her own cousin, Elizabeth, was going to be the mother of this man, of Saint John the Baptist. When the Blessed Virgin heard this she forgot all about herself, through pleasure at hearing that her cousin was going to be the mother of the man that was to get the people ready to hear God. I hope, dear children," concluded Sister, "that you are just as well pleased when others are honored, as the Blessed Virgin was."

*Questions:* 1—What else did the angel Gabriel tell the Blessed Virgin when he visited her? 2—Was the Blessed Virgin glad to hear of the honor given Saint Elizabeth? 3—How do you feel when others are honored?

## 83. A Visit of Love

"You bet the Blessed Virgin was pleased to hear that her cousin was going to be the mother of the man who was going to get the people ready to hear Our

Lord." So spoke Norman White to a number of his friends after school was out that day. "Why, she was so pleased that she started out on a long trip to see her cousin, and to tell her how happy she was to find out that her cousin was honored."

"I guess you know what her cousin said when she met her," said Eugene Stafford.

"Yes, I did know, but I forget."

"Why, she said that the Blessed Virgin was the most blessed of all women and that her Son, Jesus, is the most holy of all men. We say the same thing when we talk to the Blessed Virgin in the 'Hail Mary.' Don't you remember that we say, 'Blessed art thou among women, and blessed is the fruit of thy womb, Jesus'? Well, when we say that we are saying what the Blessed Virgin's cousin said to her."

I tell you, dear children, that all the boys were glad to hear that, and whenever they said the "Hail Mary" after that, they always thought of the Blessed Virgin's visit to her cousin.

*Questions:* 1—What did our Blessed Mother do to show that she was pleased at the honor given Saint Elizabeth? 2—What did Saint Elizabeth say when she saw her? 3—Did you ever hear those words before? 4—Now tell me what the angel Gabriel said to the Blessed Virgin, and add what Saint Elizabeth said to her.

## 84. Saved by a Mother

A man had just been caught trying to rob a store. The owner of the store was terribly angry. He was ordering the police to take the man to jail. The thief tried to say that he was starving, and that he had had nothing to eat for many days, but the owner of the store would not listen to him. Just then the mother of the owner came into the store. She looked at the thief; she saw how thin he was; she begged her son not to have him arrested; to be satisfied if he promised never to steal again. At first the owner of the store did not want to listen to his mother. Finally, however, he told the officers to leave the man go, if he promised never to steal again. The man was not long in making that promise, and he was set free. He had been saved by the mother of the storekeeper.

*Questions:* 1—Is it right to be angry when others hurt you? 2—Do you think the storekeeper would have done right to send the thief to jail? 3—What do you think made the storekeeper's mother ask him to let the thief go?

N. B.—For teachers' helps see page 214.

### 85. Mary's Request

When Our Lord had grown up He went with His mother one day to a wedding. The wedding was in the house of a great friend of theirs. While dinner was going on Our Lord's mother noticed that there was not enough wine to serve all the people who were there. So she asked Our Lord to help them. Did He refuse her? Indeed not. He told the servants to fill the pitchers with water, and then to give that to the people who were at dinner. The water was changed to wine, because the Blessed Virgin had asked Our Lord to help her friends.

*Questions:* 1—Why did Our Lord change the water into wine? 2—Did He give us any example there? 3—Do you think your mother is happy when you do what she asks? Why?

### 86. Sons and Mothers

Harriet Fink was interested in the story of the thief who was saved by a mother's prayer. She thought

over it, and thought some more, and finally she got the
answer. The answer was to be found in this, that
sons love their mothers.

"I suppose," she said to her little girl friends, "that
is why Our Lord changed that water into wine when His
mother asked Him to. I know He must have loved
her more than any son ever loved his mother, because
He could see how good she was much better than
others."

*Questions:* 1—Why ought sons love their mothers? 2—
Why do you think Our Lord loved His mother more than we
love ours? 3—How can we show that we really do love our
mothers?

## 87. An Unending Love

Hannah Tucker had listened to what Harriet was
saying.

She soon joined in and said, "Yes, and Our Lord
loves His mother just as much now as He did then;
and if He changed water into wine for her then, He
will listen to her now, too. If she asks Him to forgive a thief, or anyone who has done other kinds of
bad things, He will listen to her. You can just bet.
I know how much power the Blessed Virgin has, and
when I pray I always ask her to get Our Lord to give
me what I want."

*Questions:* 1—Was the storekeeper's mother like the Blessed
Virgin in any way? 2—Do you think the Blessed Virgin wants
to help us? 3—How can she help us?

## 88. The Blessed Virgin's Help

"I suppose you think that you're the only one that
asks the Blessed Virgin to help you," said Regina

Whelan after Hannah Tucker had said she prayed very often for the Blessed Mother's help. "Why we all do," continued Regina. "At the end of the 'Hail Mary' we all say, 'Holy Mary, Mother of God, pray for us sinners, now and at the hour of our death.' When we say that we ask her to go to Jesus in Heaven and ask Him for the things we need. We ask her to do that now and especially when we are going to die."

*Questions:* 1—When do we all ask the Blessed Virgin to help us? 2—What do we want her to do for us? 3—When do we tell her that we want help?

## 89. A Prayer to Mary

"I know the 'Hail Mary' already," said Martha Snyder as she ran into her home from school. Daddy took her on his lap and asked her if she knew what the different parts meant.

"Oh! certainly, daddy!" answered Martha. "The first part is what the messenger told the Blessed Virgin when he told her she was going to be Mother of God. The second part is what her cousin, Saint Elizabeth, the mother of Saint John the Baptist, said to her when she visited her. And the last part is what we say to her when we ask her to go to Jesus to get help for us."

Daddy was pleased to find that Martha knew so much about this prayer in honor of the Blessed Virgin and he promised Martha that to reward her, he would have Father Collins say a Mass for her that week.

*Questions:* 1—What two visits does the "Hail Mary" remind you of? 2—Why do we say the "Hail Mary?" 3—Do you think Martha Snyder's reward was worth having?

## VIII. THE OMNIPOTENCE OF GOD

### 90. Where Did the Robin Come From?

Suppose someone should introduce us to Mr. and Mrs. Robin. After we would talk with them a little while we could find out their first names (because robins have first names just as we do). Then we would like to know where their home is. They would tell us that they had come from many miles away, down in the beautiful warm South, where the sun shines. But how did the robin get there? Where did the robin come from in the first place? The robin came, just as everything here on earth comes, from God.

*Questions:* 1—Where did the robins come from just before they came to see us? 2—Who made the robin? 3—Do you thank God for making the robin for you?

### 91. My Robin Friends

I like the robin. I like the robin because God made him. I like Mr. and Mrs. Robin and all the little baby robins because they come from God. But God made the little robins just to live here on earth. He wanted them to sing, and hop, and chirp, and make little boys and girls happy. That was all he made them for. But God made me for something more than that. He wants me to sing, and pray, and make others happy, too. But He wants to give me something better than all that. He wants me to go up to Heaven and be happy there, after I am through living here on earth. God has been more generous to me than to the robins. I must not forget to thank Him.

*Questions:* 1—Do you like the robin just because he sings or for any other reason? 2—What did God intend the robins to do when He made them? 3—What does God intend you to do?

N. B.—For teachers' helps see page 218.

## 92. The Grass Carpet

When we were introduced to Mr. and Mrs. Robin the first time, where did we find them? They were dancing around on the grass, were they not? Oh! how much more soft the grass is for them than the hard ground. Did you ever walk on real, soft carpet, especially when your feet were sore from walking far, or from wearing tight shoes? Didn't it feel pleasant? Well, the grass feels just like that to the feet of the robins. No wonder they seem so happy to be playing about on it.

*Questions:* 1—Do you know where the carpet in your house comes from? 2—Do you think the robins like to walk on the grass carpet? 3—Do you think they thank anyone for giving them that carpet?

## 93. The Maker of the Robins' Carpet

I wonder who made the robins' carpet? We know the robins did not go to the carpet store to buy it. Before Mr. and Mrs. Robin came to our neghborhood, we had a white carpet (all of snow). Then suddenly, it seemed as though someone knew that Mr. and Mrs. Robin were coming to visit us, and spread this beautiful green carpet so they would be comfortable. I am sure you know who spread this carpet and who made it. Why, the same Person that made the robins. God made the robins, and He made the beautiful carpet for them to dance upon.

*Questions:* 1—Who made the white carpet and the green carpet on the ground? 2—What all have you heard lately that God has made? 3—Can He make many things more?

## 94. The Maker of Our Furniture

Did God make the carpets in our houses just as He made the grass carpet for the robins? I know there are some little children who think that just because their parents go down to the store to buy the carpets and the furniture they have in their homes, that God did not make those things. Where did the material come from for the carpets, if it didn't grow on bushes, or stalks, or even on animals? And who put it on the bushes, or on the stalks, or on the animals, if it wasn't God? And where does the wood for our furniture come, if it doesn't come from trees? And who made the trees if it wasn't God? Yes, dear children, all our carpets and all our furniture come from God just the same as the robins' carpet. Will you thank Him?

*Questions:* 1—Who makes your furniture? 2—Tell why you think you ought to thank God for your furniture? 3—Does God do the hammering and the sawing? What does He do?

## 95. A Saint Who Made Furniture

Of course, when we get our carpets and our furniture, they are all made to look fine because different men take knives, and scissors, and hammers, and nails, and saws, and get the stuff that grows, ready for us to use. We could never use the cotton that grows on bushes for a carpet unless some men had made it look fine, then made threads of it, then sewed it together. We could never use trees for chairs and tables, unless some man took his saw and sawed them up into boards, then nailed the boards together, then painted them for us. But unless God had given us the cotton and the trees to start with, the men would have had nothing to work on. But God did not want to give us everything ready to use. He wanted us to do some work ourselves. So these men who get our carpets and furniture ready are doing what God wants them to do. That was what Saint Joseph did. You remember how he took care of Our Lord when he was just a little baby. Well God chose him to be His protector just because he was a good furniture-maker. You can be loved by God if you do your work well as Saint Joseph did.

*Questions:* 1—Does God want the men to hammer and nail and saw and sew? 2—Will He reward them if they do this work for Him? 3—Tell me someone He did reward for such work? 4—What kind of work does God want you to do now?

## 96. Unlimited Power

James Shanahan and Frank McCutcheon were watching a carpenter working on the porch of James' home. They were very much interested in the way he sawed the different strips of wood, and nailed them one to another. When James' mother called him, he did not want to leave off watching the carpenter work.

As he went to obey his mother he said to Frank: "I just love to see people make things, don't you? I like to see painters painting signs, and window-trimmers trimming windows, and carpenters making wooden things. My! but I would be interested in seeing how God makes things. But He makes them in a second. Everything we see, the flowers, the trees, the animals were made by Him; why even we ourselves were created by Him, and just in a second, too."

"I hope," said Frank, "that you do not forget that God made you much better than the animals; that He made you to be happy with Him in Heaven after you had served Him well down here on earth."

Frank was only saying what he knew to be true. He knew that James did love God and was trying very hard to get to Heaven by being good down here.

*Questions:* 1—Does it take God long to make things? 2—Does He make very many things? 3—Why did He make you?

## IX. THE HOLY TRINITY

### 97. The Robins' Prayer

When Mr. and Mrs. Robin go out looking for breakfast, they do not forget where that breakfast is to come from. They are not so busy looking for things to eat that they forget to chirp. They do that to make others happy. You know how much you like to listen to the chirping of the robin, don't you? Well, God likes to hear it just as much as you do. Those chirps are the morning prayer of the robin. It is the only way the robin can say good things about God; it is the only way the robin has to say, "Thank you," to Him. But the robin uses that way and chirps and chirps and chirps. Are you going to allow the robin to treat God better than you?

*Questions:* 1—Why do the robins chirp before breakfast? 2—Do you think God likes to hear the robins chirp? 3—What does He like to hear children do before breakfast?

### 98. The Song of the Robin

I'll bet you wonder why the robin chirps three times before it looks around, but I am just going to ask you to try to figure out the reason yourselves. What did we say the robin is doing when it chirps? We said it was praying, didn't we? Yes, that was it. The robin in chirping is saying its morning prayer. And when anyone is praying you know as well as I that he is talking to God. But how many Persons do we talk to when we talk to God? Why, to three Persons; to the Father, the Son, and the Holy Ghost. We say their names when we make the Sign of the Cross. Now the robin chirps once for each of them. That's why it chirps three times before it looks around.

*Questions:* 1—What do you do when you pray? 2—To how many Persons do we talk when we talk to God? 3—Why does the robin chirp three times?

N. B.—For teachers' helps see page 221.

## 99. Three Divine Persons

We know that the robins are right in talking to the Father. It is to Him we pray when we say the "Our Father." We know that they are right in speaking to the Son. We heard many good things about the Son already. We heard that He came down from His home in Heaven just to save us. We saw how good He was as a little Babe. We learned that He is really and truly in church waiting for us to come and see Him. So we know that the robins are right in talking to Him. He is God, too. We are sure that the robins are doing right in talking to the Holy Ghost. We know that, because God the Son told us when He was here on earth, that the Holy Ghost is God just the same as He and the Father are.

*Questions:* 1—Have we heard about the Father already? 2—What did the Son do for us? 3—Who told us about the Holy Ghost?

## 100. Three in One

The Father, the Son, and the Holy Ghost, each is God and yet there is only one God. This we know because Christ who died to save us told us, and He can not tell a lie. Once a great saint was trying to tell some people how this could be. He saw a little clover growing by the road, and he picked it up. There was just one stem but there were three leaves all attached and growing together. He said to them,

"You see how these three leaves all make one leaf; let that show you that the Father, and the Son, and the Holy Ghost make only one God." But, dear children, we don't need the leaf, do we? We take the word of God, the Son, for it, don't we?

*Questions:* 1—Did Our Lord say there are three gods or only one God? 2—Do you believe Him? 3—What kind of a leaf shows how there can be three Persons in only one God?

# X. THE CONFITEOR

## 101. The Snow Departs

When the snow goes away the little blades of grass are happy, and the flowers, too, are pleased, and they feel, oh! so thankful to spring for having come to chase the cold of winter away. A long time ago Heaven became cold and chilly when that proud being who had no body became so smart that he turned against God. All the good beings in Heaven felt terribly cold, just as we do when winter and the snow is here. But just as spring chases away the winter and the snow, so a beautiful and powerful being or messenger of God gathered with him all the good messengers and chased

that awful proud being out of Heaven so that everything could be bright and warm again. That good messenger's name was Saint Michael—and all boys who
have that name are supposed to be like him.

*Questions:* 1—What made Heaven cold long ago? 2—Who
made Heaven warm again and how did he do it? 3—What
makes our hearts cold towards God?

## 102. Protectors of the Infant Church

"Do you know why the robins build a nest?" Sister
Robert asked her class just after they had read the
lesson about the mother and father robin making their
home in the tree. "Why, I am sure you ought to know
that it is to take care of the little blue eggs from which
the baby robins are going to scratch their way later on.
They build to protect them. I suppose, though, that
you do not know that God appointed twelve men whom
He called Apostles to take care of the people who believed Him. These men took care of the people right
after Christ ascended into Heaven. They were just
as careful of their people as Mr. and Mrs. Robin are
of their eggs. Their head and leader was Saint Peter,
who was the most careful of all, because God told
him that he was to answer for all who wanted to get
to Heaven."

*Questions:* 1—Why does the robin build a nest? 2—What
did Our Lord appoint the twelve Apostles to do? 3—Who was
the leader of the Apostles and what did he do?

## 103. Mrs. Robin and the Thief

"One time," said Gerald Shea, "I saw a robin sitting on a nest and I knew there were eggs in it.

While I was watching, I saw a snake climbing up the trunk of the tree."

All the children shivered when Gerald mentioned the snake.

"I suppose Mrs. Robin saw it at the same time that I did, because she started to shriek, and shriek. All of a sudden I saw Mr. Robin come flying through the air. As soon as he had come, both of them started to peck at the eyes of the snake. It was not long until the snake turned around and made off as fast as it could."

All the children were pleased to find that the eggs were saved.

*Questions:* 1—Did Mrs. Robin run away from the snake? 2—What would have happened if she did? 3—How did she protect the baby robins?

### 104. Persecutors of the Early Church

Father McCormick heard about the story of Gerald's, and the next time he came into Gerald's class, he told them about some who, though men, acted very much like that snake who tried to steal the robin's eggs. You know there were twelve men told to take care of the people who loved Christ, and who were living when He died. Well, all of them, and especially Saint Peter, tried very, very hard, and they did what Christ told them. But some bad men tried to scare them and to steal the good people away from them and from Our Lord. They killed many of the good people and all of the twelve men, except one. But the more they killed, the more the good people listened to those of the twelve men who still lived, and to others whom they appointed before they died. Just as the snake could not steal the eggs, so the bad men could not steal the good people away from Our Lord.

*Questions:* 1—What did the bad men try to steal? 2—Who acted like Mrs. Robin when she saw the snake? 3—Did the bad men hurt the Apostles? What did they do to them?

## 105. Saul, the Enemy of Christ

Father McCormick went on to say that there was one man especially who did all he could to steal the good people, and to make them bad. He became so good at finding out where these good people were that he went from city to city, just like a detective, to show the bad people where the good were. One time, though, he was holding the coats of some of the bad men when they were throwing so many stones at one of the good men that they killed him. That good man's name was Saint Stephen, and he prayed for all those who were killing him. And his prayer did a whole lot of good, for the man who was holding the clothes soon became a good man himself.

*Questions:* 1—Did Saul love the Christians or hate them? 2—What did Saul do when the bad men were stoning St. Stephen? 3—What did St. Stephen do while he was being stoned?

## 106. Paul, the Friend of Christ

"Oh! I know who that was," said Frank Ganter, as he and his friends were leaving school. "Yes, I mean I know who it was that held the coats of the bad men while they were stoning Saint Stephen. That was Saul. I know the whole story. You know a little later, he was going on horseback to a different town when he was thrown off his horse, and when he tried to look around he was blind. He heard a voice saying, 'Why are you persecuting me?' He knew right

away that it was God talking and he promised to quit
hurting the good people and to be one of them himself.
He was told to go into the nearest town, and take instructions.  When he went to the priest, his sight came
back.  He became a Catholic, and a very good friend
of Christ.  That was what Stephen's prayer did for
him.  Believe me, that sure is a good way to get even
with your enemies.  I'm going to pray for mine, too,
just to show them that they can't make me angry."

*Questions:* 1—Did Stephen's prayer help anyone? 2—What
made Saul turn to be a good man? 3—Has Stephen's prayer
taught you anything? What?

### 107. Journeys for the Faith

When Frank told this to his sister at home, she surprised him by telling him that she knew all about it.

"And," she said, "he was just as strong in helping
the good people afterward as he was bad to them before.  He wasn't afraid of anything.  Disease didn't
bother him; swords, why he'd just look at them and
laugh; the ocean, he was always on it, traveling from
one place to another, trying to tell as many people as
he could about the good things Our Lord had bought
for them when He died on the Cross.  And talk, why
he could keep the sleepiest person awake for hours at
a time.  It's no wonder that so many people learned
about Our Lord from him.  Finally, he was killed also,
like so many of the other good people, just because he
was a friend of Our Lord.  Now, I guess you think I
didn't know anything about Saint Paul, for that was
Saul's name after he became Christ's friend," said
Clara, as she walked away, proud that she was not
behind her brother in knowledge.

*Questions:* 1—Name some of the things St. Paul was not afraid of? 2—Why do you think he was a brave man? 3—How is St. Paul like St. Stephen?

## 108. Father Hackett's Friend

"Ah! you go and ask him, Matt, he won't refuse you. You know he likes you."

The boys wanted a free afternoon to play ball and they knew they couldn't have it unless Father Hackett gave them permission. They were afraid he would refuse it unless they sent some one whom Father Hackett thought a great deal about. So they thought, and thought, and finally decided that Matt Sweeney was the boy to go. Matt was just a little afraid, but finally consented to go. And the boys were right—Father Hackett gave them permission.

*Questions:* 1—Would you like to ask something of somebody you had offended? 2—Would you be afraid to ask anything from someone who loved you? 3—Why do you think the boys were wise in sending Matt to see Father Hackett?

## 109. Friends in Heaven

Our little friends, Harriet Fink, Hannah Tucker and Regina Whelan, heard about Father Hackett giving the boys a half-holiday, because each one of them had a brother on the ball team. You know it was they who were speaking about how easy it is for the Blessed Virgin to obtain gifts for us from God.

"But," said Regina, "we have other friends in Heaven, who are also friends of Our Lord. Do you forget about Our Lord's cousin, Saint John the Baptist.  I guess a cousin ought to be able to get things for you."

"Yes," said Harriet, "and there is Saint Michael who chased all the bad people out of Heaven, so it would be a nice place to stay.  I guess he ought to be able to get some things, too."

"You all forget Saint Peter, who took the most care of Our Lord's friends after His death, and Saint Paul, who traveled all over the world you might say, just for Our Lord.  I guess they ought to have something to say, too, when it comes to getting favors for us."

*Questions:* 1—Name some of Our Lord's friends. 2—Tell something you have heard about each one in the stories you have just heard.  3—Why do you think they will be able to do for us what Matt did for his friends?

## 110. An Appeal to Friends

Father Smith was in the sitting-room, having called to see Mr. Whelan, when this discussion took place.

"Dear children," he said, "don't you start any argument about this, because you all ask those saints and the Blessed Virgin, too, to pray for you when you say the 'Confiteor.'  First you stand before them and God, and say that you have been bad; then, showing that you need their help you ask them to pray to God for His blessings."

I tell you Mr. Whelan was glad that Father Smith was visiting him at the time, because he settled everything so as to please all three little girls.

*Questions:* 1—Why do you think it was a good thing Father Smith had called to see Mr. Whelan? 2—What is the first thing you do in saying the "Confiteor"? 3—What do you ask your friends to do in the "Confiteor"?

### 111. Father Smith's Demonstration

But Father Smith did not stop with that. He wanted to show the little girls that what he said is true.

"You tell how bad you have been to God and your friends when you say, 'I confess to Almighty God, the Blessed Mary ever Virgin (that's your first friend), to Blessed Michael, the Archangel, (your second friend), to Blessed John the Baptist (your third friend), to the holy Apostles, Peter and Paul (your fourth and fifth friends), and to all the saints (all your friends put together), that I have sinned.' Then you ask them to pray for you when you say, 'Therefore I beseech them to pray to the Lord, our God, for me.' "

I tell you that those children were glad to hear that every time they say the "Confiteor" they are talking to friends in Heaven, and they were more anxious to say it after that.

*Questions:* 1—Name the friends you confess your sins to in the "Confiteor." 2—Are your friends ashamed of you when you confess your sins? 3—Which one of these friends do you love the most?

## XI. THE RESURRECTION

### 112. Daddy's Return

Catherine Ferry was patiently waiting for her daddy to come home. If any little girl loved her daddy, that little girl was Catherine. If any little girl knew how hard daddy had to work, that little girl was Catherine. And if any little girl knew how many good things daddy had given her, Catherine knew. She enjoyed daddy's return from work for it gave her a chance to show him how much she loved him. Whenever he was late she worried, thinking that perhaps an accident might have taken him away from her. He was a little late tonight. Shortly, however, she heard daddy's step upon the porch. You can bet she was glad.

*Questions:* 1—Why do you think that Catherine Ferry obeyed daddy? 2—What did Catherine do when daddy came home from work? 3—Why was she worried when daddy was late coming home?

### 113. The Rose Bush

When you see a beautiful red rose in summer time do you ever stop to think how it grew, and became so handsome? Once upon a time there was no rose bush upon which that rose might grow. One sunny morning saw that bush push its little head above the ground where before nothing had grown. Long before that a little seed was placed in the ground, and died there; and when it died the beautiful rose bush commenced to grow. So from the dead seed came that beautiful rose of which you think so much.

*Questions:* 1—When the seed died did it give life to something else? 2—What helped the rose bush to push its head above the ground? 3—Who made the rose grow from the buried seed?

N. B.—For teachers' helps see page 224.

### 114. Jonah's Escape

A long, long time ago God spoke to a very holy man named Jonah and told him to go to preach to some people who were very, very bad. But Jonah was afraid and he tried to escape his duty by sailing away in a boat from his own country. But God followed him, and sent a storm which rocked the boat to and fro. Jonah knew what caused the storm, and he told the men on the boat to throw him overboard. They did. He was not drowned, however. A big fish came and swallowed him, bringing him safely to land after three days. Believe me, Jonah was always careful to listen to God, and to do what God told him after that.

*Questions:* 1—Can we escape doing what God wants us to do? 2—How does the story of Jonah give you the answer? 3—What makes you think that Jonah's sin in running away was forgiven him?

## 115. Rebuilding a Temple

You know what a temple is. A temple is another name for a church. Well, if you just stop to think how big a church is, you will know that it would take a long time to build it. Just stop and think how many bricks would have to be put together and how many men would have to work on it.

Well, one day when Our Lord was walking around telling men what to do to be saved, and to be good, some one said to Him, "Why should we listen to you? You have never done anything wonderful!"

That was a terrible thing to say to God and it's a wonder God did not strike him dead.

He simply said, "Destroy this temple and in three days I will rebuild it."

In only three days! Did He keep His promise? We shall see.

*Questions:* 1—Why did Our Lord allow the people to talk so mean to Him? 2—What answer did He give them when they insulted Him? 3—Do you think He can do what He said? Why?

### 116. A Hope

After Our Lord died on the cross, they wrapped him up in sheets and buried Him in a grave. Then His friends felt terrible. They felt worse than Catherine Ferry would have felt if her father had met with an accident. But it was not long until their sadness left them. You know I told you that Catherine waited patiently for daddy. So the friends of Our Lord waited for Him. They knew He was in the grave, but still they felt that He would come to them again. He had told them so many times about the great things they were supposed to do, that they could not help think He was coming back.

*Questions:* 1—Whom did the Apostles feel like when Our Lord was buried? 2—Was Our Lord their Father? 3—Did they wait for Him as Catherine awaited her daddy?

### 117. The Empty Grave

Our Lord's friends felt so bad about His leaving them that they could not keep away from the grave. He died on Friday, and on the next Sunday morning as they came to the grave, they saw that it was empty. But what do you think! There was an angel, a messenger from God, sitting near the grave. Were Our Lord's friends frightened? Would you be frightened, if you were there? They were still more astonished, however, when the angel told them that Our Lord was alive again, and that He would see them and talk with them, and walk with them again. But they were very happy over it, too. They were even more happy than Catherine Ferry was when her father came home from work. Our Lord is more than a mere father; He is God.

*Questions:* 1—What made Our Lord's friends go to the grave on Sunday? 2—What did they find at the grave? 3— Why were they glad to hear what the angel said?

### 118. A Thoughtful Boy

Paul Hughes was a very thoughtful boy. When he heard the stories you have been listening to during the last few days he connected them all together. The dead seed coming to life in a beautiful rose reminded him of Our Lord rising out of the grave, beautiful and bright. Then he remembered that Our Lord was in the grave three days and three nights just as Jonah was in the big fish that long. And he didn't forget either that Our Lord promised to rebuild the church in three days.

"I know what church He meant," said Paul. "He meant His own body. He meant He would make it come to life three days after death."

Finally, Paul saw that Our Lord's return was not unlike the return from work of Catherine Ferry's father.

*Questions:* 1—What did Our Lord's coming out of the grave remind Paul of? 2—Did you ever hear stories about such things? 3—Did you think they ought to remind people of Our Lord's coming out of the grave?

### 119. A Great Power

After Our Lord was placed in the grave, His friends were very much afraid of the people who had put Him to death. They kept out of the streets as much as possible. Only once in a while would any one go to His grave, as we saw some going three days after His death. One day while Our Lord's friends were gathered together in a room He came in, without even opening the door. You may be sure they were glad to see Him. He told them that He was going to give them a great power, the power to do what He had been doing, the power to forgive others' sins. He wanted them to be able to chase the devil away and to make people ready for Heaven. Then he left the room but He met His friends many, many times after that.

*Questions:* 1—Why were Our Lord's friends afraid? 2—How did Our Lord come to them in the room where they were hiding? 3—What power did He give them there?

### 120. A Visitor for Forty Days

"I wonder how many know how long Our Lord stayed visiting His friends after He came back to life," asked Sister Frederick of her class one day.

Little Martin Smith put up his hand right away.

"How long, Martin?" asked Sister.

"Six weeks," answered the boy.

"Are you sure it was that long?" asked Sister again.

"Well not quite that long; it was two days less, just forty days."

"Well, what happened after those forty days were up?" asked Sister.

"Why He went back to His home in Heaven."

*Questions:* 1—How long did Our Lord stay with the Apostles? 2—Do you think they wanted Him to leave even after that? 3—Where did He go this time when He left them?

## XII. THE DESCENT OF THE HOLY GHOST

### 121. Lonely Again

All the people loved Jesus.  So when He left them after His visit of forty days, they were very, very lonely again.  But He promised them before He left them that He would send them a great helper.  How long do you think they had to wait?

"I know, I know, Sister," said Philip Kelly, when his Sister asked his class that question.

"Well, how long, Philip?" asked Sister.

"Just a few days over a week," answered Philip. "Just ten days."

"Well, I wonder who it was that came to help them," said Sister as she thought aloud.

"Why, the Holy Ghost came.  He came in the shape of tongues that were burning, as a sign that they were going to be able to preach real well, and make other people love Jesus just as they had loved Him."

*Questions:* 1—How long after Our Lord's going into Heaven were the Apostles lonely?  2—Who came to them then?  Is that Person God?  3—Why did He come in the shape of tongues that were burning?

### 122. Two Constant Visitors

"So we have two visitors with us always," said Ruth Murphy to her little friend, Jean Harkins.  "We have the Holy Ghost, the Third Person of the Trinity, really and truly God, whom Our Lord sent to stay with us and make us holy; and we have Our Lord Himself in Church, waiting for us to come and talk to Him, waiting to have us tell Him our troubles."

"My!" said Jean, "we ought to be very good. I did not know till today that the Holy Ghost is interested in us. Now I'm going to thank Him over, and over again for coming to tell the good things I must do, and I'm going to thank Our Lord, too, for having Him come, first a long time ago to His friends, and now to all of us."

*Questions:* 1—Is the Holy Ghost with us always? 2—What other visitor is always down here on earth waiting for us to come and talk to Him? 3—Why ought you to be grateful for these Friends?

### 123. Three Great Feasts

"I'll bet you don't know on what day we remember Our Lord's coming out of the grave," said James Brown to Patrick Sweeney, his cousin.

"Yes, that's right, I'll bet you don't," chimed in Terence O'Reilly, the chum of both of them.

"Say, don't insult me like that," said Patrick. "Why we remember Our Lord's coming out of the grave on Easter Sunday."

"Well, what day do we remember His going back to Heaven?" asked Terence.

"Is this an examination?" asked Patrick. "But if you think I don't know I'll tell you. Forty days after, on Ascension Thursday, which is a holyday, we remember His going up to Heaven. I hope you don't forget to hear Mass on that day. Now I'm going to ask you a question, Terence. What day do we remember the coming down of the Holy Ghost?"

"Ask me something hard, why don't you?" answered Terence. "Ten days after Ascension Thursday gives us Whit-Sunday. That's the day we remember the coming of the Holy Ghost."

*Questions:* 1—When does the Church remember Our Lord's coming out of the grave? 2—When do we remember His going up into Heaven? 3—When do we remember the coming of the Holy Ghost?

## XIII. HOLY COMMUNION

### 124. Unselfishness of Mr. and Mrs. Robin

After the little baby robins scratch their way out of the little blue eggs they are very, very weak. They can not fly, because they have no wings; they can not look for worms, because their feet are so weak that they can not stand on them. Here is where mother and father robin show how much they love the little robins. When mamma finds a nice big worm, she does not keep it all to herself; she brings it home to her babies. When daddy finds a nice grasshopper, he does not say, "Here is a fine meal for me;" he brings it home for the little baby robins.

Children, you should learn from this unselfishness of the robins to be kind to your playmates. You ought to be ready to share with them the things with which God has blessed you.

*Questions:* 1—How does mother robin show that she is not selfish? 2—How does daddy robin show it? 3—How do the robins teach you a lesson?

### 125. Mother's Helper

Mother robin is kind to her babies, but your mother is much more kind to you. Do you ever stop to think how much trouble it is for a mother to stand before a hot stove, day after day, just to have nice things ready for her little children to eat. Hedwig thought it was no trouble at all until one Christmas when she got a wonderful set of pots and pans for a present; she tried to make some mashed potatoes in her little pot. She had to peel the potatoes; watch them while they boiled; mash them; add milk, and butter, and salt; and then mash them some more. When she was through, she said,

"O mamma! how tired and overheated I am! Do you always get tired when you get our meals?"

Mother said she did, but that she was glad to do that for her little children. Hedwig promised to be more kind to her mother after that, and to help her with the dishes after every meal.

*Questions:* 1—Why would you not like to be like Hedwig before she got her present? 2—Why do you think it was a good thing Hedwig got her present? 3—Do you think children ought to be kind to their mothers for working for them?

N. B.—For teachers' helps see page 228.

### 126. Money for Food

"If daddy did not work hard, we never would have anything to eat. Mother would have nothing to cook if daddy did not get the money to buy things with. Just think of her going to the market without any money. She couldn't pick up things for nothing like the robin can find worms, and grasshoppers, for the little baby robins."

"Yes," said her brother, "and daddy has to work terribly hard to earn that money. I was through the mill with him where he works, and you ought to see the heavy iron rods he has to lift. And hot! well I think I was soaking wet when I got out!"

"Yes," said Grace, "I know that daddy works hard,

not for himself but for us.  That's the reason why I
always try to be good to him."

"And I, too," chimed in her brother.

I hope, dear children, that you treat your daddies the
same as these two children did.

*Questions:*  1—Is mother the only one that works so we can
eat?  2—How does daddy help to get us our meals?  3—How
should children show their daddies that they thank them for
their work?

### 127. The Young Pelicans

The mother robin feeds her baby robins by hunting
worms and insects for them.  She shows how pleased
she is to help these poor little babies out.  Still, she is
not nearly so willing to help her robins as was a
mother pelican to help her babies, in a story that I
heard.  Mother robin many times must go hungry in
order that the mouths of the little ones in the nest may
be filled, but she does not injure herself to feed them.
This mother pelican, however, cut herself with her
beak, and from the blood that flowed from the wounds,
the young were fed.  From it they got the food that
was necessary to make them grow up into birds, beautiful as their mother was.

*Questions:*  1—Who can tell me once more what the robin
feeds the baby robins?  2—What did the mother pelican feed the
baby pelicans?  3—Is the robin or the pelican more unselfish?

### 128. A Thoughtful Teacher

William Conner had a dream one night.  He had
been studying his reading lesson very hard.  In his
reader he had seen a picture of a great crowd of peo-

ple sitting around a man with a long garment on, with flowing hair, and a short beard. This same thing came to his mind in his dream. He could actually hear the man speak. As he watched him he knew that it was Our Lord. Shortly after Our Lord finished talking, His friends started to pass around bread and fish to the people. But they didn't give William any. He was so small that they could not see him. But Our Lord called him to His side and gave him all he needed to eat. He woke up just as he was about to eat. I tell you he was the happy boy to think that Our Lord had actually given him food.

*Questions:* 1—Why would you have liked to have been William Conner? 2—What would you have said in your dream to Our Lord? 3—Can you say the same thing now? Will you?

### 129. Bread from Heaven

A long time ago, even before God came down from heaven, God's special friends were moving from one country to another. They were in the desert, where nothing was growing. Indeed, they were very hungry and they thought they were going to starve to death. But God, being their special friend, would not forget them and so He sent down from heaven some very sweet bread. It came down very much in the same way that rain comes down from the sky. It fell every morning, except Sunday. The people went out with baskets and collected enough to keep themselves and their children alive.

*Questions:* 1—How did God feed His special friends in the desert? 2—When did this food fall? 3—What did Our Lord want to teach the people by not sending food on Sunday?

N. B.—For teachers' helps see page 231.

### 130. The Passover

Once God's friends were trying to get away from a bad King who was making them do all kinds of hard work. The King did not want them to go. But God showed the King that he would have to let the people leave, by punishing the King and the other bad people. Finally after a child had died in every family except in the families of God's friends, the King was glad to get rid of the people who had caused him to be punished. No sooner were they gone than he was sorry he had let them go, and he went after them with his soldiers. God's friends kept ahead of them, till they came to a big sea. Then they thought they were caught. But God told the leader of His friends to stretch a rod over the sea. When he did a dry path appeared, and the people crossed over it. When the bad people tried to get across, the water closed in on them and drowned them.

*Questions:* 1—How did God make the King allow the good people to go away? 2—What did the King do after the people had started? 3—How did God save the people?

### 131. Celebrating a Feast

The Jews, who were God's friends, always celebrated their getting away from the bad King every year. They had a banquet, but at the banquet all they had to eat was roast lamb, crackers, and lettuce, because that's all the people ate before they started out on their trip when they left the bad King. And on that day they had to eat standing up, with their traveling clothes on, because that's the way the people stood, and that's how they were dressed, on the day they ran away from the bad King, who had been making them work so hard.

*Questions:* 1—How did the Jews remember to thank God every year for saving them from the bad King? 2—Why did they eat the things they ate at the feast? 3—Why did they wear the things they wore?

### 132. Christ and the Passover

Now, as Our Lord's mother was a Jewess, He did the things that the Jews were supposed to do. He was glad, therefore, to celebrate this feast, by which God's friends honored Him for helping them across the big sea. The very night before He died was the night on which the Jews honored God, by the banquet we have told you about before. Our Lord knew He was going to die. But that did not make Him do any different than the rest of the Jews. He sent some of His special friends to get a hall ready for Himself and His twelve helpers. After everything was ready Our Lord went to the hall where the table was ready, and with His twelve friends ate the roast lamb, and crackers, and lettuce, standing up, and dressed in traveling clothes.

*Questions:* 1—What did Our Lord teach us by celebrating the feast in memory of the saving of the Jews by God? 2—How did He know that He was to die next day? 3—Do you treat your enemies as Our Lord treated the Jews who were going to crucify Him?

### 133. A New Food

But after Our Lord with His friends had finished celebrating the feast which the Jews held in honoring their escape from the wicked King, Our Lord looked and saw Himself on the Cross and He said to Himself, "How shall I feed them when I leave them?"

He knew that He would continue to feed them, because He had fed His friends many, many years before, when He sent down bread from heaven into the desert, and He loved these friends just as much as He did the ones who were traveling through the desert. And He had promised just a short time before that He would give them food from heaven, and God will never go back on His promise. The only thing that was to be figured out was *how* to feed His friends.

*Questions:* 1—Did Our Lord love the friends that were in the desert more than He loved those who were at the table with Him? 2—Why couldn't He go back on His promise? 3—What was that promise?

### 134. Caroline Hall's Picture

Caroline Hall was only six years old but she knew very much about her religion, because her mother had been kind enough to teach her. In the dining room of her home there was a very long picture. It was a picture of a big, long table with thirteen people sitting at it. In the middle of the picture was Our Lord and on each side of Him there were six of his friends. One day, Caroline's little girl friend, Ellen Fries, came in to pay her a visit.

After the two little girls had played jacks for a while Ellen looked up at the picture and said, "O Caroline! Do you know what that picture means? I saw one just like it in the store, and I have been wondering ever since what it might stand for."

"Why," said Caroline, "that's a picture of 'The Last Supper.' It shows us Our Lord celebrating the feast in honor of the escape of the Jews from the bad King. You know it was at the Last Supper that

Our Lord gave us Himself as food to be received in Holy Communion."

*Questions:* 1—What do you know about the picture that was in Caroline's home? 2—Did you ever hear before this of what Our Lord was doing in that picture? This story told you something new about what Our Lord did at the "Last Supper." What is it?

### 135. The Institution of the Blessed Eucharist

"You know," continued Caroline, after the children had finished their game of jacks, "that after everything had been done as the Jews wanted it done, Our Lord took some of the bread that was on the table, and blessed it, changing it into His Body, and giving it to His friends to eat. Then He took the chalice in which there was wine, and blessed it also, changing it into His Blood, and giving it also to His friends. I tell you they must have been afraid at first to eat and drink, after they knew what looked like bread and what looked like wine were no longer bread and wine, but the Body and Blood of Christ, instead. But Our Lord told them to eat and drink, so they obeyed. So also He tells us to receive Him, and we do so when He comes to us in Holy Communion."

*Questions:* 1—When did Our Lord give us the new food, Himself, in Holy Communion? 2—How did He show the Apostles what to do in giving Holy Communion to the people? 3—Did the Apostles receive Holy Communion at the Last Supper? 4—What did Our Lord change bread and wine into?

### 136. A Transferable Power

"How can we receive Our Lord in Holy Communion?" asked Ellen, who had not yet received any instructions about receiving Our Lord. "I thought you said that Our Lord gave what looked like bread and what looked like wine just to His friends. How does it come that there is a chance given us after this long, long time, to receive Our Lord just as they did?"

"Oh! that's easy to answer," said Caroline. "You see He gave the power He had to His friends, and told them to give that same power to all the priests they would send out to take care of His other friends. Why, don't you know that He wanted to give Himself to all His friends, as food to keep them good?"

"No," said Ellen, "I did not know that; but since you have told me, I can hardly wait to receive Him."

"Oh! never mind," answered Caroline, "as soon as you make your First Holy Communion, you may receive Him every day if you want."

*Questions:* 1—How does it come that the priest can change bread and wine into Our Lord's Body and Blood? 2—Why does God want to give us His Body and Blood? 3—When do you receive Our Lord? 4—Do you want your soul clean or dirty when Our Lord comes to it?

### 137. Like the Pelican

Hubert Richards heard the story of Caroline and Ellen, and after it had been entirely told he said to his mother, "Oh! Our Lord is just like the mother pelican in the story. Sister told us the other day about a mother pelican who fed the young pelicans from her own blood, and here we have Our Lord giving us Himself for food. Doesn't it remind you of the bread that came down to feed the Jews when they were in the desert? Only that was mere bread. Our Lord gives us not bread merely, but Himself. I am glad you told me about Caroline and Ellen, mother," he added, "it has made me love Our Lord more than I ever did before."

*Questions:* 1—How does the pelican feed its young birdies? 2—How does Our Lord feed us now? 3—Does the pelican remind you of Our Lord? 4—Is Our Lord more unselfish than the robin, than your mother and daddy? Why do you think so?

### 138. A Bad Boy

Frank Bennett had been told many times by his mother that he ought not to bother the poor robins who were trying as hard as they knew how to protect their little blue eggs, so that the baby robins might grow and finally break through the shells. But Frank knew too much for his mother. So one day in the spring he spied a robin's nest in one of the trees that grew a short distance from his home, and he began to climb just purposely to get the eggs he thought were in the nest. As he climbed, the wind grew harsher and harsher, but Frank paid no attention to it. As he got closer to the nest it became windier and windier. Finally, just as he was about to reach for the eggs, a terrible gust of wind shook the tree; Frank lost his balance, fell, and broke his arm. When he was carried into his home, the doctor came and bandaged his arm. But I'll tell you something—Frank never tried to rob a nest again. Just think, too, how good the wind was to the robins.

*Questions:* 1—Did Frank deserve what he got? Why? 2—Why do you think God loved the wind? 3—Do you think the robins thanked the wind?

N. B.—For teachers' helps see page 234.

## 139. Playful Towser

Towser was too old to hurt anybody. But just the same when he would run at you you would think he was going to chew you up alive. Little Bertha Huber was visiting the Leroys, where Towser lived. And when the little girls commenced to play with Bertha, Towser thought he would join in the fun; so he growled, and growled, and ran right at Bertha. My! but Bertha was scared; but Towser was only laughing to himself. What do you think Bertha did? Why she ran right to her mother's arms. And Towser quit chasing because he was afraid of Bertha's mother.

"Now, just for that, Towser," said Mrs. Leroy, "you go into the woodshed and stay there until the company goes home."

Towser did not like that a bit, but he deserved it for showing off when there was company present.

*Questions:* 1—Why do you think Towser deserved what happened to him? 2—Who protected Bertha? 3—Which is the better protector, mother or the wind?

N. B.—For teachers' helps see page 237.

## 140. Prayer for Protection

"You ought to see how big the ocean is," said Thomas Shaw to his friend, William Morris, after he had returned from a trip on the ocean. "My! Bill, you can't even see a bit of land anywhere. And when the wind blows, the water rushes against the ship just as though it were trying to push it over into the sea. One night, especially, there was a terrible storm. It rained, and rained, and rained; and the wind blew so hard that the water was coming up on top of the ship.

We were all afraid. But there was a priest with us. He gathered all the Catholics together, and we said the Rosary. We had just finished about one-half of it when the storm came to an end. I'll tell you that some of the Protestants were so surprised at that, that they decided to take instructions and become Catholics."

*Questions:* 1—Who has charge of the storm? 2—Who would you think can stop it? 3—What do you think of the Catholics who prayed? Were they preaching?

### 141. Christ and the Storm

After William Morris had heard Thomas' story, he invited him over to his house.

"I want to show you a picture," he said.

When they arrived at William's house, William took Thomas into their living room and pointed to a picture on the wall.

"I guess," said he, "that the storm was something like that."

"Yes," said Thomas, "only I don't think we were in so much danger because our boat was a steamboat; and that boat is just a weak little boat with sails."

"Yes, but look who's in that weak little boat."

"Oh! that's different. I wouldn't be afraid if I were in that boat."

"But the men who were in it were; you know that well enough."

"Yes, I know that they thought Our Lord didn't know there was a storm just because He seemed to be asleep. They woke Him. Then, He said, 'Why were you afraid? Don't you know that I could protect you even if I was asleep?' Then, He reached out His hands, and the winds stopped blowing, and the waves rolled less high, and the storm was at an end."

*Questions:* 1—Did Our Lord know what was going on when He was asleep? 2—Would He allow anything to happen to His friends? 3—Why did He feel bad when they awakened Him?

## 142. A Robber of Souls

"You know," said Paul Carr, "the more I think of that bad boy who tried to rob the nest of the birds, the more I think of that bad spirit that was chased out of Heaven."

"Well, why don't you call him by his right name?" asked Henry Carey.

"Yes, I mean the devil. He's always trying just as hard as he knows how to rob Heaven. I mean he wants to get people to do bad things so they won't get there. And he does it just because he hates God, and is jealous of everybody that wants to do right. Believe me, though, it's a good thing we have somebody to protect us, just as the wind protected the robins. Christ who chased the storm away when the boat of His friends was in danger will chase the devil away from us. But in order to have Our Lord near us always, we must remember to receive Him in Holy Communion as often as we can. Then, we won't need to fear the storm."

*Questions:* 1—Who is trying to rob our souls from God? 2—Who will protect us as the wind protected the robins? 3—How can we have Him with us in our hearts, to protect us, every day?

## 143. Worse Than Towser

"I could not help thinking of the devil when I heard about Towser running at Bertha Huber as though he were going to chew her up." This was what Clara Finn told her friend, Marie Jacques, as they were going home from school one day.

"I don't see how that made you think of the devil. Towser couldn't hurt anybody; but the devil can."

"That's just it; the devil can't, unless we want him to. We have to help him to hurt us, if he is to do us any harm. Unless we do bad ourselves, the devil can't do a single thing. Our Lord took all his teeth away when He died on the Cross. I agree with you that the safest thing to do is to fly to the arms of Our Lord when the devil is after us; that's the surest way to keep from helping him out when he wants to hurt us. We should fly to Our Lord by visiting Him often in church, and by receiving Him every day if possible in Holy Communion."

*Questions:* 1—If the devil lost his teeth, how can he bite so many? 2—Who will save you as Bertha's mother saved her? 3—What is the best way of flying to Our Lord's arms?

## 144. Storms of Temptation

Matthew Casey could not forget the story of Christ and the storm. He had never seen a storm on the ocean, but he had heard the wind howling around his home on cold winter nights. And to think that those winds would stop blowing just as soon as Our Lord stretched out his hand! That was wonderful, indeed. The more he thought the more he compared the winds and waves with the whisperings of the devil. He knew that the devil tries to drown our souls through coaxing us to do bad things. He felt sure, however, that the hand of Christ which had chased away the storm will chase away the temptations of the devil, if we only ask Him to do it. He knew that the best way to have Christ with us to chase the devil away from us is to receive Him as many times a week as we can in Holy Communion.

*Questions:* 1—Do you think Matthew's comparison a good one? Why? 2—Would we be drowned if Our Lord would not help us out of temptations? 3—Wouldn't it be a good idea to have Our Lord with us every day, to still the storms in our souls?

## XIV. CONFESSION

### 145. Not Asleep

Fred Carson and Michael Feldman were talking about the picture representing Christ stilling the storm at sea.

"It does seem funny, doesn't it, Fred, that Our Lord's friends thought He was asleep?"

"Oh! there are lots of people just as bad nowadays," said Fred. "When they have trouble, or get sick, or make mistakes, or get low marks, or get scolded, they just cry, and get angry, and feel bad all over. They forget that Our Lord is with us. Just because they can't see Him, they forget that He is really and truly in our Tabernacles, before which the little light keeps burning, watching that we won't get hurt. And oh! how pleased He is to have us come and tell Him we are not afraid of anything, because we know He is on guard to save us."

*Questions:* 1—Are there any people afraid as the Apostles were? 2—Can even those who do not receive Holy Communion every day, place their trust in Our Lord? Where should they go to do so? 3—Which is better, to receive Our Lord every day, or just to visit Him in church every day?

### 146. The Sunbeam's Obedience

Way up in the sky with mother sun lived a beautiful little sunbeam that was oh! so anxious to get down to earth to see what there was to be seen there. But mother always told the sunbeam to wait, that soon there would be work to be done on earth and that then she would send her little sunbeam down to do it. Finally, after the little sunbeam had obeyed her mother patiently for many, many days, mother sun told the little sunbeam to hurry up and go down to the little old building that sat in the yard right below them. Maybe that sunbeam wasn't happy. She hurried all the way down.

*Questions:* 1—In what two ways was the sunbeam obedient? 2—Do you think Our Lord loved the sunbeam? Why? 3— Does the obedience of the sunbeam teach us anything?

### 147. The Sunbeam's Promptness

As soon as the little sunbeam was told to go down to the little old house with a secret message, she started out.

And as she passed the clouds, they shouted, "Come, little sunbeam, come and play with us. Come, let us have some fun."

But the sunbeam politely refused because she knew she had other work to do.

And as she passed the little birdies flying through the air, they cried to her, "Come, little sunbeam, come and play tag with us. It really is the best game you ever knew."

But again the sunbeam politely refused. And as she passed the tree top, the tree invited her in to rest awhile, but the sunbeam simply told the kind old tree that she must be on her way. It is no wonder that Jesus loves the sunbeams when they are so prompt as this little sunbeam was.

*Questions:* 1—What three chances had the sunbeam to stop on her way down to earth? 2—Give another reason why Our Lord loves the sunbeams. 3—What lesson have you learned from the sunbeam's promptness?

### 148. The Sunbeam's Perseverance

When the little sunbeam arrived at the building to which she was sent, she tried to get in, but could not because the blinds were all down. She knocked, and knocked, and knocked, and still no sign was there that the blinds would be lifted. Anyone else would have been discouraged and would have just made up his mind to go home and have no more to do with an old house where the people were not polite enough to let you in. But not so the little sunbeam. She just made up her mind that she was going to do what she had been sent to do, even if she had to stay there all day and all night, too. She kept on knocking until finally the blind was raised and she skipped into the room, full of joy and ready to do her work. I wish all little boys and girls would be just as anxious to perform their duties as this little sunbeam was.

*Questions:* 1—Do you get tired when you can't learn to spell a word right away? 2—Do you think the sunbeam would get tired over that? 3—Will you be like the sunbeam after this? Why?

### 149. The Sunbeam's Cheerfulness

What do you think the sunbeam found when she entered the room? Just what her mother, the sun, had told her she would find. The room was almost bare. In it there was just an old chair, an old table on which were piled a lot of medicine bottles, and an iron bed on which there was lying a little girl, named Ida McCune, who was terribly pale and sick. In fact, the doctors all said that she could never be well again. Ida knew this, and she felt terribly sad. But the little sunbeam would not believe what the doctors had said. She told Ida not to be sad, that she felt sure she was going to be well. That was what she was sent to tell Ida. She stayed, and played with Ida until night time, when it is time for all good little sunbeams to be in bed. But she left happiness behind her; and in about three weeks Ida was up and walking about her room. I think the sunbeam was a very fine doctor, don't you?

*Questions:* 1—Would you like to stay in that room where the sunbeam stayed? 2—How was the promptness of the sunbeam shown in this story? 3—How will you cheer the sick?

### 150. The Rosebuds' Wishes

Once there grew side by side in a garden two rose bushes. On the one grew red roses, and on the other, white. Now it happened that on either bush there was a bud just as old as a bud on the other. One bud was, of course, red; the other, white.

The red rosebud began to talk to the white rosebud and asked, "What do you want to do when you grow up?"

"I," asked the white rosebud, "why I want to help the poor. They never get any beautiful flowers, and I want to go to them and make them happy."

"Well, you surely are a foolish little rosebud," said the red rosebud knowingly, "you'll never be happy with the poor. I would never think of going to a poor person's house. I want to go to the rich where they have lots of music and dancing. That's what will make me happy."

Which rosebud do you think, dear children, you would like the better?

*Questions:* 1—Which do you like more, the red or the white rosebud? 2—Why does the wish of the white rosebud remind you of the sunbeam? 3—What do you think of the red rosebud's reason for wanting to go to the rich?

### 151. The Wishes Fulfilled

After the rosebuds had grown up to be real beautiful roses, the gardener came around one afternoon and cut them from the bush. After he had his basket filled with roses, he sent them to the flower store where people go when they want to buy flowers. While they were in the store they kept on wishing just the same things they had wished in the garden. One day, a beautiful automobile stopped in front of the flower store, and a very rich lady with a long handsome seal coat came into the store, and ordered a dozen bouquets of red roses. As she was leaving, she passed a priest who came in and ordered just one bouquet, but a bouquet of white roses. This bouquet was to be sent to a little girl who was suffering from scarlet fever. I know you don't have to ask me in which bouquet the white rose wanted to be placed; nor where the red rose wanted to go. It just happened that the florist put the red rose in one of those twelve bouquets; and the white rose in the bouquet for the sick little girl.

*Questions:* 1—Do boys and girls sometimes wish things like the red rosebud? How would they wish it? 2—Who sometimes lets them have their wish? 3—Why do you think He allows it?

### 152. The Red Rose's Adventure

When the red rose was brought to the home of the rich woman, the delivery boy had to go around to the back door, because packages were not taken at the front. That was a shock to the red rose already. Then when she found that the servants were the ones ordered to arrange the bouquets in vases for the table, she felt hurt again. Finally, the bouquets were all ready, and the table set, and the word was given that dinner was served. Soon all the people in their fancy dresses came in and sat down. Then the servants brought in soup. The woman who was sitting just behind the bouquet in which our friend, the red rose, was placed, must have been very awkward, because, just as she was going to eat of her soup, she dropped her spoon. As she stooped to pick it up, she pulled the table cloth with her, and the whole bouquet fell into her soup. The bouquet was taken out and thrown away. That was the end of the red rose.

*Questions:* 1—What was the first thing that spoiled the red rosebud's happiness? 2—Do you think the rich people paid much attention to the red rose? 3—Do you think that something will happen to boys and girls who wish to be rich, similar to that which happened to the red rose? What might happen to them?

### 153. The White Rose's Adventure

The white rose was taken with the white bouquet to the sick room where Angela Friend was lying ill of scarlet fever.

When she saw the beautiful flowers she said, "Oh! how kind Father Feeney is to think of me!"

Then she took the bouquet and hugged it very close to her.

Afterwards, she looked at all the flowers in it, and picked out our friend, the white rose, saying, "Mother, put the others in a vase and place them on the table near me, but I am going to keep this one, to hug and hug and hug. Oh! mother I'm sure I am going to get well, now. This little rose is cheering me up more every time I look at it."

That night when the doctor came he thought a miracle had been worked. He could not understand how it was that Angela's fever had gone down so quickly. The mother pointed to the white rose. I tell you that white rose was proud. Now, dear children, which rose do you think was the happier? What is going to be your wish?

*Questions:* 1—Which received the more attention, the white rose or the red? 2—Who do you think rewarded the white rose for her good wish? 3—Did the white rose remind you of the sunbeam? How?

### 154. The Kindness of the Pink Rose

Once upon a time a pink rose grew in the corner of a pretty garden. It was a very beautiful rose. And it was just as kind as it was beautiful. One day it spied a poor, little bumble-bee, looking half dead.

"Oh!" said the bee, "I'm nearly dead, I have been looking all day for honey, but I never knew it to be so scarce. I have none after all my work, and I know that I am too weak to go any farther. I am too tired even to go home."

"Well, I'll give you a rest for the night," answered the pink rose. "Just crawl inside my petals, and get a good drink of honey, then lie down and go to sleep. In the morning I am sure that you will be perfectly well again."

Was that little bee glad? Well, I believe that's a foolish question. In the morning the bee felt just as well as ever, ready and fit for work again.

*Questions:* 1—Does the pink rose remind you of the robin? Of your mother and daddy? Of the pelican? Of Our Lord? How? 2—What sermon do you think the pink rose preached to you? 3—How are you going to show the pink rose that you can be just as good as it?

## 155. One Good Turn Deserves Another

About three days after the pink rose helped the bee, something dreadful nearly happened to it. It was not yet old enough to be cut off the bush, yet some bad boys saw it and wanted it for themselves. So, they got an old knife, ready to cut the pink rose off the bush on which it was growing. The rose saw this and trembled away down to the very bottom of its soul. But it couldn't stop the boys from doing what they intended. It had forgotten its act of kindness to the bee a few days before. Just as one of the boys was about to cut, the rose heard a buzzing sound; then it heard the boy scream, "Ouch!" and drop the knife. The bee had stung him, and returned the favor he had received from the pink rose.

*Questions:* 1—If someone did a good turn for you, would you pay him back? 2—How are you paying back mother and daddy and Our Lord for the good turns done you? 3—Will you allow the bee to be more grateful than you?

## 156. Trixie in Trouble

Madeline Foley had a little dog named Trixie. Trixie had a habit of snapping and barking at other dogs. Madeline spoke to him very seriously one day and told him that he must not do that; she threatened to punish him if he did. Trixie listened very attentively but I really do not know what was in his mind because he did not pay attention to Madeline very

CONFESSION 131

long. The very next day, he saw a big shepherd dog passing the house, and he ran out and barked just as before. The shepherd became angry, turned around and snapped back, and kept going on his way. But that snap had been an awful one. Trixie received a terrible bite, and ran back into the yard, howling and howling as though he were dead. Madeline ran out, and when she saw the wound, she knew what had happened. She did not punish him. She took good care of the wound, washed it daily, and in a week it was all healed again. I tell you Trixie had learned his lesson. He did not snap at other dogs any more.

*Questions:* 1—How was Trixie's disobedience punished? 2—Did Madeline forgive him? 3—How do you know she forgave him?

N. B.—For teachers' helps see page 241.

## 157. The Runaway Lamb

Once upon a time in a flock of sheep there was a little lamb who was very, very curious. This little lamb was not satisfied to follow the shepherd along with the other sheep. It ran away as often as it got a chance. Its mother scolded, and the shepherd scolded. But still the lamb would stray. One day, when it saw a chance to get away from the flock, it ran, and ran, and ran. It was running so fast that it did not see a hole in the ground just ahead, and soon it was slipping, slipping, down deep into the hole. There it lay, sick and sore, wondering whether it would be left there to die. It seemed like years before it heard the shepherd's voice. My! but that voice was welcome! The shepherd came, and took the lamb upon his shoulders and brought it back to the flock. It had broken no bones, but it was stiff and sore all over. The shepherd nursed it until it got well again.    The lamb, too, had learned its lesson, and never ran away from the flock again.

*Questions:* 1—Is the straying lamb like Trixie?  How?  2— What punishment did the lamb receive?  3—How do you know that the shepherd forgave it?

N. B.—For teachers' helps see page 245.

## 158. The Sorry Chick

Once a mother hen was watching over her little chicks when she saw one of them going over near a pond of water where the ducks were swimming.

"Don't you dare to go near that pond," said the mother hen, "you can't swim; and if you go into that pond you'll surely drown."

The little chick seemed to be listening attentively and the mother hen thought that it would surely obey. But what was her surprise just an hour later to see her little chick slip into the pond.  The hen ran all about the yard clucking in great terror.  And the chicken maid, who saw what was going on, ran over and saved the little chick from the water.  The mother hen was glad to see her chick safe; and watched over it until it was perfectly dry.

*Questions:* 1—What do you find alike in Trixie, the stray- ing lamb, and the disobedient chick?  2—What would have happened if the chicken maid had not been near?  3—How do you know that the mother hen was like Madeline and the shepherd in forgiving?

N. B.—For teachers' helps see page 249.

## 159. Mabel's Misfortune

Mabel was acting like her brother, trying to make a wooden whistle with a penknife.  She was getting

along fairly well until the knife slipped, and she cut
her finger. When she saw the blood, she cried and
cried. The first thing she thought of was to run to
mother. That she did. Mother assured her that the
cut was not that serious; then Mabel felt more at ease.
Mother got some iodine and painted the cut with it;
then she bandaged it well; and in a few minutes Mabel
was going about the house singing to her dolly as if
nothing had happened.

*Questions:* 1—Did Mabel think her mother was a doctor?
Why do you say so? 2—Did Mabel's mother love her? How
do you know? 3—Would your mother do for you what Mabel's
mother did for her? 4—Ought you not, then, love your
mother?

### 160. The Doctor's Kindness

"That little girl must be pretty sick," said James
Harder to his friend, Michael Ritter, as they were gaz-
ing at a picture I am sure most of you have seen. It
shows the doctor sitting watching attentively a little
girl who is lying either asleep or unconscious upon a
bed in a very poorly furnished room.

"I'll bet she is," answered Michael, "but it's a good
thing the doctor is there. Say, it's a good thing we
have doctors to take care of us, isn't it? I know that
no doctor can be as kind as mother. But then mothers
don't have time to study like doctors. So they can't
always tell what's wrong with you. Believe me, I always thank the doctors for being so kind to us."

*Questions:* 1—Do doctors know how to cure better than
mothers? Why? 2—Which is the better nurse, mother or
the doctor? 3—Are you grateful like Michael?

### 161. Better Than a Doctor

"Yes, but a doctor has to come back to your house a whole lot of times to make you well. He has to send your daddy to the drug store to get all kinds of medicines, that old bitter stuff, before you can get well. I guess a doctor is not as good at curing people as someone I know." This was what James said to Michael after the latter had expressed himself as thinking a great deal of doctors, and as thanking them very much for being so good and kind to people.

"Oh! I know whom you mean," answered Michael, "I agree with you that He was a much better doctor. But then He was God. You don't need to think that I forget about Him, James. When I praise our doctors, I praise Him also, because He's the one that made the doctor bright enough to know what's wrong with you. So when the doctor cures you, it's really God that's doing it."

*Questions:* 1—Does it take doctors long to cure? 2—Who cured people in an instant? 3—Who makes the doctor cure us?

### 162. Cured in an Instant

"I just got my glasses, today, Ella," said Sarah McLean to her chum, Ella Lambing. "Do you know it makes the biggest difference in the world. Everything looks quite different to me now."

"Well, if just getting a pair of glasses makes such a big difference, what do you think it would be like to be cured of blindness? Say, I would like to have been present when Our Lord cured the two blind men; just in a moment they got their sight. I tell you they must have been astonished—and thankful too."

*Questions:* 1—Do glasses make people see better? 2—Why do you think the blind men would thank Our Lord? 3—How did His curing them show He was not a mere human doctor?

### 163. A Parent's Prayer

Once upon a time, about nineteen hundred years ago, there lived in Jerusalem, a man who had a son who could never learn anything. He was always forgetting things. He even forgot that it is dangerous to get near the fire. Many times he got so close to the fireplace that he would come close to being burned up. Indeed, he would have been burned many times, only his father saved him. The doctors all said that they could not do anything for him. But one day, the father heard of the greatest doctor that has ever been here on earth. The father took the boy to Him and explained what was wrong with him. In a moment, the boy was cured and he became perfectly well. That doctor was Our Lord, who came down from Heaven just purposely to take care of us.

*Question:* 1—Whom else did Our Lord cure in an instant? 2—Why do you think of Our Lord when you think of the sunbeam, the white rose, Madeline Foley, the shepherd, the mother hen, and the doctor, about whom you have heard during the last few days?

### 164. A Doctor for Body and Soul

Geraldine Carlton was very sick with measles, and she was tired of being in bed. Mother came in to her room one evening and told her the story of the forgetful boy being cured by Our Lord.

"He is ready to cure you, too, if you only ask Him," said her mother.

"Oh! indeed I know that," said Geraldine, "and I am ashamed of myself for forgetting about it. Indeed, I remember about how quickly Our Lord cured a man that was very sick with his nerves. His nerves were so bad that he could not keep still. His friends brought him lying on his bed to Our Lord. At first, instead of curing him of his nervous trouble, Our Lord told him that his sins were forgiven. My! how the people wondered at that. They could not understand, because they did not know that He is God. But He soon showed them that He could forgive sins. He proved it by curing the man of his nervous trouble. After that, most of the people believed that He really could forgive sins; and we believe it, too, don't we, mother dear?"

*Questions:* 1—Does Our Lord cure only the body? What else does He cure? 2—How did He prove that in the case of the man with bad nerves? 3—Which should you be most anxious to have cured, body or soul?

## 165. Doctors for the Soul

Geraldine's mother reminded her that Our Lord still forgives people's sins.

"Indeed, I know that," said Geraldine. "Don't I know that just as He has left Doctor Sheppard to cure me of my measles, so He has given me Father Baney to cure my soul and take my sins away."

"Do you know when He left the priest the power to take your sins away?" asked mother.

"Yes. After He arose from the grave, He appeared to His friends one day, when the doors were all locked, and He told them that they were to have exactly the same power as He had, and that they could pass that power on to others just as He was passing it on to them.   I tell you, mother, I am going to remember, all during my sickness especially, to thank Our Lord for giving us these doctors to cure our souls."

*Questions:* 1—How does Our Lord cure our souls now?   2—What is the difference between the doctor and the priest?   3—When did Our Lord give the priests the power to cure souls?

## 166. Vincent Reflects

"The priest," said Vincent Fallert, "is like the sunbeam we heard about a few days ago.   Just as the sunbeam brought cheer to the sick girl, Ida McCune, and helped her to get well, so the priest comes promptly to us when our souls are sick, I mean when they have sins on them.   He may scold, but that's only to keep us from getting our souls in the same condition again. And when we have gone to confession, we feel cheery and bright again, because the sunbeam, the priest, has cured us through the power he received from Christ."

*Questions:* 1—To what did Vincent compare the priest?   2—Why did he make that comparison?   3—Why should you go to the priest in confession?

## 167. Mighty Like a Rose

Pauline McVey and Helen Shannon were walking through Helen's garden one day when they spied a rose bush growing close to the fence.

"Oh! the beautiful roses," said Pauline.   "May I have one?"

"Why certainly," said her friend, "here, take this white one."

"By the way," said Pauline, "do you remember the story of the white rose and the red?   You know, about the roses that wanted to go, one to a rich house, the other to some poor person.  Well, you know, I have been thinking that the priest is very much like the white rose.  With all his education he could very easily go to the houses of the rich, but he prefers to go to the poor sinners who want their souls cleaned, who want to get well again.  So he sits and sits and sits, and hears confessions just to make people strong so that they can fight the devil away, just as the white rose made Angela Friend strong enough to fight away her fever."

*Questions:* 1—Why is the priest not like the red rose?  2—Why is he like the white rose?  3—When the priest wants to help you will you refuse?

### 168. A Port for the Shipwrecked

"Yes," said Helen, "and I have not been able to forget the story of the pink rose and the protection it gave to the poor little bee that was all tired out from looking for honey.  You remember that the rose invited the bee to crawl right within its petals, to drink honey, and to rest there.  Well, I have thought over and over again how much that rose is like the confessional.  The tired soul goes in there full of sin (which is the cause of its being tired), drinks there of the honey which God pours into the soul to take away sin, and comes out feeling fine; as the bee was good and strong the next morning after its night of rest."

*Questions:* 1—Why is the sinful soul like the tired bee?  2—What does it need to make it strong again?  3—Where can it get it?

### 169. Like Trixie

After Madeline Foley had received instructions about confession, she said to her chum, Stella Whiteside, "You know, I think boys and girls are pretty much like Trixie. They just try to be bitten by the devil, just the same as Trixie snapped and barked at that big shepherd until he turned around and bit him. But it's a good thing that we have somebody to wash that bite and cure it, even as I cured Trixie's bite. Otherwise, blood poison would kill us. I mean that if we did not have confession, where the priest washes away our sins, we would soon find our souls dead, and not long after, buried in hell."

*Questions:* 1—Why are boys and girls like Trixie? 2—Why is the priest like Madeline?

### 170. A Shepherd of Souls

"Well," said Stella, "I heard a story of a little lamb that was very much like Trixie. That lamb always ran away whenever it got a chance. The result was that one day, it fell down a big hole in the ground and would have died there, too, only the shepherd ran after it and saved it. I think boys and girls are like that lamb, I mean some boys and some girls, who are bad. They run away from the shepherd who is the priest, when they commit sin; of course, as soon as they do that they fall down the hole the devil has dug for them. And they would stay in that hole, too, if it were not for the priest coming after them and rescuing them by forgiving their sins in confession."

*Questions:* 1—How was the little lamb like Trixie? 2—How is the priest like the shepherd? 3—What lesson have you learned from this story?

### 171. The Mother Hen's Forgiveness

After Harold Franz had heard the story of the mother hen and the disobedient chick, he wondered and wondered and wondered. He could not understand why the mother hen was so anxious to take care of the chick after it had been disobedient and tried to swim. He said so to his mother.

"Why, Harold," answered she, "that ought not to be hard for you to understand. You see the priest doing that when he forgives people's sins. He is always telling them to be good, but some of them are bad. When they are bad, however, he is only too glad to go and forgive their sins, to take care of them, because he loves them."

*Questions:* 1—Why do you think the mother hen took such great care of the chick that had disobeyed her? 2—How does the priest remind you of that mother chicken? 3—Would you be afraid, then, to tell to the priest the bad things you have done?

### 172. Reformation

Patrick Lavelle had heard the stories of Trixie, and of the straying lamb, and of the disobedient chick. He thought it was a lucky thing for them that they had some one to take care of them. He was glad to hear that they obeyed after they had learned their lesson.

"I can't understand," he said to his mother one afternoon, "why boys and girls don't learn their lesson. Here God is good enough to take care of them after they have hurt their souls, the priest forgives them, and still they do the same thing over again."

*Questions:* 1—Why does the priest remind you of the sunbeam, the white rose, the shepherd, the mother hen, Madeline

Foley, and the doctor, about whom you have heard recently?
2—Did the animals cared for by Madeline, the shepherd, and
the mother hen, learn their lesson? 3—Do people whom the
priest forgives always learn their lesson? Are you going to be
like those who do not?

### 173. Sorrow

"I have often noticed that, too, Patrick," answered
his mother. "It may be because they do not feel really
sorry for their sins. Anybody that is really sorry for
what he has done would never do the same thing over
again. You know that, don't you?"

"Sure, that's just what I'm getting at. Suppose a
boy takes an apple from the fruit stand and is caught.
He tells the man he is sorry and won't do it again.
The man lets him off. As soon as the man's back is
turned he takes the apple again. I know that if the
man saw him do it again, he would be arrested. That
boy certainly wasn't sorry. So when a boy goes to the
priest and says he is sorry he must be sure that he is
not going to do it again. Otherwise God just looks
on his confession as a mockery, and his sins are not
forgiven."

If Patrick could have seen his mother's eyes at that
moment, he would have wondered what was wrong.
She was crying because she was proud of Patrick. She
thought sure that he would be a priest when he knew
so much about confession already.

*Questions:* 1—Is one who is truly sorry going to do the same
thing over again? 2—How did Patrick show that? 3—If one
is not sorry, how does one look at his confession?

N. B.—Certain commandments and precepts have been chosen
for consideration in the next five stories. For explanation of
choice see Introduction, page 23.

### 174. Lawrence and His Sister

"I'm never going to quarrel with my sister again," said Lawrence Finneran to Walter Murphy, his cousin.

"So you're sorry for being bad, and you're going to be different, are you?"

"Yes, because I always get the worst of it; mother always believes everything that Ruth says, and after every quarrel I get a whipping."

"Why, I am surprised at you, Lawrence. Is that the only reason you are sorry for your quarrelling? Don't you ever think that God loves your sister and that when you hurt her you hurt Him?"

"Well, what does she sass me for, then?"

"That's her sin. If she hurts you, you won't straighten things out by quarrelling. Be really and truly sorry, Lawrence, in the right way. Be sorry, because when you quarrel you hurt God."

*Questions:* 1—Why was Lawrence sorry? Was he sorry in the right way? 2—Do you think that God liked Lawrence's sorrow? 3—If you had been Lawrence, would you have been sorry?

N. B.—For teachers' helps see page 252.

### 175. Michael Goes to Mass

"You can bet I'm never going to be kept in after school on Monday afternoon for missing Mass again. You have to stay in a whole hour and a half; and if you went to Mass you would get out in three quarters of an hour." This was what Michael Rogan said to Charles Flanagan, on their way home from school one Wednesday afternoon.

"Is that the only reason why you are going to go to Mass on Sunday, because you are going to be kept in after school? Is that the way you are going to treat

God after what He has done for you, coming down to stay in church to help you? I guess you don't care about committing a sin, do you? You don't care about slapping God in the face, either, saying, 'I'm not going to do what You want.'"

Michael tried to answer, but he was so sorry for what he had said and done that his voice trembled and he could not.

*Questions:* 1—Why did Michael make up his mind not to miss Mass? 2—Why wouldn't God like that reason? 3—Why do you want to go to Mass every Sunday?

N. B.—For teachers' helps see page 256.

### 176. Martin's Good Friend

"Come on, let's get a pear," coaxed Martin Fowler as he tried to get his chum, Carl Meyer, to steal some fruit.

"Now just wait," said Carl. "Suppose your daddy gave your brother a pear. Would you take it right out of your brother's hand while your father was looking and watching what you were doing? I don't think you would, because you know that you would be punished for it, if you did."

"Well, my daddy didn't give the fruit store those pears!" answered Martin.

"No, but God gave them to the owner of the store. And He is watching you right now; and if you take away from the owner of the store what God gave him, you will be punished for it just as you would be punished for stealing from your brother what your daddy gave him."

*Questions:* 1—Who is the Father that is watching over all of us? 2—Who gave each and every one of us all we have? 3—Does He want us to steal from one another?

N. B.—For teachers' helps see page 259.

### 177. The Dust in the Song Box

"My that Victrola sounds awful," said Virginia Carpi, as one Sunday afternoon, she was listening to some records being played upon it. "I wonder what's the matter with it. Maybe the needle is old; or perhaps the record is scratched."

Daddy searched for the reason and found that there was too much dust crowded into the box where the sound comes out; as soon as the dust was removed, the Victrola played real well again.

"Virginia," said her daddy, "you know how awful that Victrola sounded before we got the dust out, don't you. Well, that's the way our voices sound to God when we are using them the wrong way. And we use them the wrong way when we do things that He has told us not to do. If a little girl tells a lie, or talks about her little friend, or says nasty words, her voice sounds to God just as that Victrola sounded to us."

*Questions:* 1—Why is the voice like a Victrola? 2—Does God like to listen to this Victrola? Why do you say so? 3—When is God disgusted with this Victrola?

N. B.—For teachers' helps see page 263.

### 178. A Thought for Friday

"You must think that meat is poison on Friday," said Phyllis Jones to Barbara Callahan.

"That's all you know about it," answered Barbara. "We know that meat is just the same on Friday as on any other day. Only we are told not to eat it on that day. Don't you obey your mother? Well, when we are told not to eat meat on Friday, in order to make ourselves think about Our Lord dying on the Cross, we do what we are told, because we don't want to be disobedient. If we should disobey, we should commit a very serious sin."

Phyllis was astonished to hear this and she never teased Barbara any more. In fact, she thought it would be a good thing if she remembered Our Lord on Friday, too.

*Questions:* 1—Is meat poison on Friday? 2—Why don't you eat meat on Friday? 3—Why do you think Barbara did well in not getting angry?

N. B.—For teachers' helps see page 266.

### 179. Need for a Light

Charles Shanahan had lost his top. He was looking every place he thought it might be. In corners, under sofas, under bureaus, every place he peered, anxious to find the plaything that meant much to him. He was not able to find it until his daddy lent him his searchlight. Only a few moments after that Charles found his top under the sitting room sofa. Dear children, when one goes to confession, he must know his sins, and the only way he can do that is find out what sins have been committed. To do that is harder than to find a top under a sofa. One must go over every day and find what wrong was done in it. But we have a searchlight that will help. That searchlight is the assistance of the Holy Ghost. So before going to confession always ask the Holy Ghost to help you find out what sins you have committed.

*Questions:* 1—Is it hard to find things in dark places? 2—What light are you going to use in the dark places of memory? 3—How are you going to get that light before confession?

N. B.—For teachers' helps see page 269.

## 180. Examination of Conscience

Michael Cunningham told his mother that he had a questionnaire to fill out, something like his brother had to fill out when he registered during the great war. You know at that time the big boys had to tell how old they were, where they lived, what kind of work they were doing. Answering these questions was answering the questionnaire. Michael's questionnaire amused his mother. It ran like this,

"Did I miss prayer? Did I swear? Did I miss Mass? Did I disobey? Did I fight? Did I steal? Did I tell lies? Did I eat meat on Friday?"

Mother knew that Michael was asking himself these questions in order to find out what sins he had committed, so that he could tell them to the priest when he would go to confession. She warned him that if he had done any of these things he must be sure to be really and truly sorry. It would not be enough just to say that you are sorry.

*Questions:* 1—Why did Michael have to get those questions ready? 2—Can you remember any of the questions he had to answer? 3—Who do you think would help him to get the right answers to those questions? 4—Would Michael have to tell how many times he had done those things?

## 181. In the Confessional

"How many know what to do when they go in the confessional?" asked Sister Clara. You would be astonished to see how many hands were raised.

"What do you do?" she asked one little boy, Mark McQuade.

"Why, you kneel down, and when you see the priest

is ready you ask him to bless you; then you tell him how long it has been since you were at confession last, and whether you said the prayers or did the things you were told to do then. Then you tell the number of sins of each kind you have committed. After that you wait for the priest's advice; and when he has given it to you, you make the 'Act of Contrition.' You must be really and truly sorry for hurting God."

Sister thought that was fine and she gave Mark a gold medal for knowing his answer so well.

*Questions:* 1—What kind of a flower did we say the confessional is like? 2—Are you going to be afraid when you go into the confessional? 3—What are you going to do when you go into it?

### 182. Before and After

"I'm always sorry after confession for the sins I have done, and I try hard to stay sorry," said Regina Haney to her mother.

"Before I even go into confession I make an 'Act of Contrition' to tell God I am sorry I hurt Him, and to promise that I won't hurt Him again. Of course, I make the same Act over again before I leave the confessional. Then after I come out, I say the penance the priest gave me, always trying hard to remember that I said I was sorry. This helps me a whole lot. You know I don't want God to think I was just fooling. So I try as hard as I know how to keep away from the sins I said I was sorry for."

"Just keep that up," said her mother, "and Our Lord will always be glad to come to you in Holy Communion, you will always be His friend, and when you leave the home He has given you here on earth, He will take you to that most beautiful home He has prepared for you in Heaven, where He will feed you every day with His love, and make you happier than any words can tell."

*Questions:* 1—In going to confession, when should you make the "Act of Contrition"? 2—How long are you supposed to remember that you told God you were sorry? 3—What will God give people who stay sorry for their sins?

# APPENDIX TO PART ONE

## Method of Development

*(Story No. 1, "The Bee That Wouldn't Leave Home," is used as an example.)*

As I was passing some beautiful flowers this morning I was thinking of you, dear children. I was saying to myself that my room is just a garden of flowers, and that all the children are beautiful flowers. I knew that God sent you to me, just as He sends the flowers into the garden.

Your bright, happy faces turn towards me when I come into the room, just as the smiling faces of the roses, and violets, and pansies turn towards God. I know why the flowers smile at God. Do you? Is it not because they are thanking Him for being so good to them? When I see your faces beaming at me, I think that you are acting like the flowers, and that you are thanking me for teaching you. I wonder if I am right. I will not ask any questions, for I want to think that it is so. It makes me happy to think so. It makes me more willing to work for all my little flowers.

Well, here I am, far, far away from the garden of flowers. Indeed, I left the garden far away when I came to school, did I not? But I mean that my story is getting far, far away from the garden. I do not want to get very far away from it, because I saw a little friend of mine in that garden. Yes, I have little friends that you know nothing about. I would be

149

rather afraid to introduce you to this friend of mine. Some people think he is not much of a gentleman; but that is because they do not understand how to act towards him. You might not like him very well. Do you think you would? Well, there I asked you a question that you can not answer. It was my fault entirely, because I did not tell you who my friend is. Now, do not be surprised when I tell you. It is Mr. Bee.

While I was looking at the flowers, I heard Mr. Bee's auto horn. That's not right, is it? Well, you know what I mean. Bees do not have horns to blow, but they can make a buzzing sound to let you know they are coming, and that you must get out of the way. Well, when I heard the buzzing, I got out of the way, because I did not want to have an accident. Mr. Bee flew right past me, as though he had never met me before. At first I felt rather hurt, but then I thought that he was trying to remember the name of some special flower to which he was to go that day. He had scarcely passed me, though, when he very cutely turned his head about, and I thought I saw him smile, though of course I may be mistaken. Then he turned around and came back, buzzing as he came. That's all he did, buzz, buzz, buzz, but I could understand pretty well, that he was telling me how glad he was to see me. A couple of times he flew very close to my ear, and I was sure that what he was buzzing was a secret just for us two; so I could not tell you what it was about.

But I do not want to disappoint you; so I will tell you about a bee who was very lazy, and who would not go out of the hive; that's the bees' home, you know. All bees must work. My little friend was going to work this morning when he stopped to talk to me. He was going to visit the flowers. They in their kindness would give him sweet drinks from their hearts, and he would turn that sweetness into honey.

Bees are very busy people, I tell you. It is best not to stop a bee, when you hear him buzzing. That's why I did not stop my friend. If they are in a hurry, they are liable to give you a sharp reminder that it is their busy day. Since bees are so busy they hate people who are lazy, especially do they hate bees who will not work. They do not coax lazy people very much either.

You can imagine, then, how the bees felt towards the bee I spoke about. At first they tried to tease him into going to work. They told him that he did nothing but snore all day, that people passing would think there was a thunder storm inside the hive. They said that his eyes looked like toy balloons, because he slept so much. They asked him if he did not think he would burst, if he grew much stouter. But that did not bother the bee. I think that if people poked fun at me like that, it would make me feel ashamed of myself, don't you?

But the bee made all kinds of excuses. He said he was not strong enough to go out to work. He was afraid that he would faint, if he had to go out in the sun, and visit the flowers. Besides he thought he ought to have a sun-bonnet to keep the sun away from his head. He did not want to be sunstruck. He told them the birds were very wicked, and as he had no sword to keep them away from him, they might come after him, and swallow him up. He also knew that if he had to leave the hive, he would miss his mother, and his sisters, and his brothers very much. He would not like to go out and work with bees, whom he had never seen before.

Did you ever hear so many excuses? I thought that lazy boys and girls were the only ones that could think of so many, didn't you? Well, the bees just laughed. They pointed to themselves, and said that if they were brave enough to go out to work, surely he ought to be so. They gave him fair warning. They told him he must make up his mind to do it very quickly. If he did not, they said, something would happen to him. The bee thought it was just a threat, and so paid no attention to them. He thought they could not kill him. He had been so lazy that he did not even know that he and other bees can sting people. Had he known that, I am sure he would not have remained idle. But it was his own fault that he did not know it, wasn't it?

One day the farmer who owned the bees came out to look at them, and to collect the honey they had made. He found the lazy bee stung to death. He knew all about what happened, although nobody told him. And he knew what kind of bee the lazy bee was, though he had not heard the story, as you have. I wonder if you know who stung the lazy bee to death, and why they did it?

God wants little children to leave home when their mothers tell them to, just as the bees wanted the lazy bee to leave the hive. God loves those children who do as their mothers tell them. Do you think He loves those children who do not? Do you think their excuses do any good? God knows the truth. I wonder what will happen to such children.

## Explanation and Analysis of Development

This is a sample of the way a teacher may develop the stories outlined in this manual. It will be noted that the story remains essentially the same, but that the points in it are unfolded before the child's vision over a longer period of time, and with the likelihood of a more nearly permanent impression. The supine laziness of the bee stands out more clearly after the diligence of bees in general is described; it is heightened in color by the ridicule poked at him by the other bees; it becomes even more stubborn in the excuses he alleges; and its extreme blameworthiness is brought out in the threat and its execution. The teacher should note that the connection between the unwillingness to leave home and laziness is brought out in the course of the story, in order to cure the child of any homesickness he may be experiencing.

The problem in developing a story is to keep the child's interest through the more extended narrative. If this sample is examined, it will be noticed that interest is sustained in the following ways:

*a.* By orienting the story to the child's experience; it is made a tale of the teacher's friends; her intimate acquaintanceship with them is shown in her learning secrets from one of them.

*b.* By asking rhetorical questions, which very often will bring an answer in the way of a nod of the head, and which will almost always recall the interest of those distracted.

*c.* By making parenthetical comments, *i.e.,* by thinking aloud; an artful way of making the child believe you are saying something you would rather not tell him; it recalls his attention, as he wants to know what teacher thinks, much more than what she says.

*d.* By introducing humor into the story; a laugh through the class will make the inattentive regret the distraction that made them miss the fun; the attentive will be on the alert for more of the same.

To show more clearly what is meant in regard to b, c, and d, it may be appropriate to quote from this accompanying development of "The Bee That Wouldn't Leave Home."

Examples of b:

1. "I know why the flowers smile at God.   Do you? Is it not because they are thanking Him for being so good to them?"

2. "Indeed, I left the garden far away when I came to school, did I not?"

3. "I think that if people poked fun at me like that, it would make me feel ashamed of myself, don't you?"

4. "Did you ever hear of so many excuses?   I thought that lazy boys and girls were the only ones that could think of so many, didn't you?"

5. "But it was his own fault that he did not know it, wasn't it?"

Examples of c:

1. "I wonder if I am right."

2. "Well, here I am, far, far away from the garden of flowers."

3. "You might not like him very well."

4. "And I thought I saw him smile."

Examples of d:

1. "Some people think he is not much of a gentleman."

2. "I heard Mr. Bee's auto horn."

3. "I got out of the way, because I did not want to have an accident."

4. "He had scarcely passed me, though, when he very cutely turned his head about."

5. "They are liable to give you a sharp reminder that it is their busy day."

6. "People passing would think there was a thunder storm inside the hive."

7. "His eyes looked like toy balloons."

8. "He was afraid he would faint."

9. "He thought he ought to have a sunbonnet."

The moral intent of the story may be indicated by the teacher or it may not. If the story has been told well, the impression of the moral will be in the child's mind of itself. The danger in pointing the moral explicitly is always that the child will feel he has been trapped. He has been enticed to listen to a story, in order to be taught. Resentment of one kind and another at this kind of treatment will dull the edge of the story, and the moral or religious purpose it had in view. His disappointment would not be unlike that of the adult who is attracted to a theatre by flamboyant advertisements, and finds that the attraction is a lecture on the "Relation between Economics and Sociology," or some similar topic, into hearing which he does not wish to be snared, though he might be willing to be informed about it, if it were candidly advertised. For this reason, it seems as a rule better when telling the story to tell only the story. Nothing can be fairer than that; that's what the teacher advertised to do. But tell the story in such a way that it will make the child think for himself, and draw from it the truth which it contains. The next day, or an hour or two afterwards, the same truth may be brought forth boldly to the class by way of review, without intimating its relation to the preceding story. The questions on the story may legitimately seek after the moral or religious point. This is to compliment the student on his ability to discover something that he was not told explicitly; and he will do his best to answer.

# PART TWO
## TEACHERS' HELPS

# PREFACE

## TO PART TWO

THE material assembled in Part Two lends itself to a variety of uses. The teacher who has the time and inclination to develop the stories by dramatizing them and in other ways will find many practical suggestions here. The thirty stories for which suggestions are given are thoroughly representative of the entire course, and the plans offered here excepting the "Silent Reading" can be adapted for all the other stories.

The primary purpose of Part Two, however, is to serve as a teacher's manual in classes where "Religion Hour: Book One. Story-Lessons in Conduct and Religion" is used as a supplementary reader in religion. In this reader, thirty stories drawn from "Teacher Tells a Story" are adapted for reading in the first grade.

Some teachers may prefer, in using both the present volume and the reader, to co-ordinate the two and arrange to have each story in the reader read by the class at the same time that the teacher gives the corresponding story in "Teacher Tells a Story." For the convenience of teachers who follow this plan, suggestions are here given as to which stories in this volume should precede and which should follow each story in the reader.

It is not expected that all teachers will be able to carry out such a plan, especially because that will necessitate the use of one comparatively brief reader through the greater part of the year. Failure to observe this co-ordination will not effect the usefulness, however, of either the reader or the present volume.

We have added some suggestions for developing the lessons, for dramatizing them, and for silent reading. They are mere suggestions, meant to make this manual more valuable to the busy teacher; they are not intended to bind the teacher whose abilities in any one of these three departments render her capable of a method that may be as good or better than that recommended here.

We have referred also to stories that may be correlated with the Reader lesson. The sources whence they have been derived are principally: Holy Scripture, the lives of the saints, history, and children's literature. It may be objected that some of these stories are too complex for the first grade. We admit the objection if the stories are to be told in complex fashion. There is no need to do this. Names and relations may be, and usually ought to be, omitted in telling them. Personal characteristics and actions, principally the latter, will suffice to make the story interesting. We refer the teacher to the method we have employed in narrating the story, "Bread from Heaven." This is a Biblical story, complex enough if it is to be told as one would tell it to an adult. It can be brought down to the child's level, however, by omitting reference to words like, "the Israelites," "Palestine," "Egypt," "manna." The purpose of stories in the first grade is not to teach history, secular or profane. History can be compelled to supply us with examples, but we are under no contract to retain names and dates that would confuse the child. What we want is the thought in the example; and this can be given the child, even though details of name, place, and time are omitted. Moreover, the teacher must not think that the outline we have given of the stories from other sources is sufficient for her effectual telling of the story, if there is time to give the complete narrative. There is nothing like a comprehensive background for telling stories in a compelling fashion. The best read men should be the best story tellers, and would be, if they would shed their pedantry. However, the sketch we give will suffice for the teacher who can conscientiously say that there is no time to consult the story in its entirety.

# PART TWO

## Teachers' Helps for Use with "Religion Hour: Book One"

*N. B.—Numeral in parentheses after each story title indicates the number of the corresponding story in Part One.*

### THE RAINDROP (5)

I am a drop of rain. My home is away up above you. It is away up above the houses, and high above the trees. I look down from my home, and see boys and girls. They are playing. I like to see them play. I should like them to come to my home, so I could play with them. I will go down to play with them when God asks me to go. God made me to do what He wants. God the Son left His home for boys and girls. He did that to make them happy. That is how I know what I must do. God is telling me now that I must go down to boys and girls. I will go.

### Related Stories in "Teacher Tells a Story."

This story should be preceded by stories 1–4, inclusive; and followed by story 6. Other stories of similar thought matter are: 57–65, inclusive; 135, 145, 146, 156–158, inclusive.

### Development of "The Raindrop."

*a.* Establish an interest contact by describing children watching the rain patter against a window pane.

*b.* Picture the dissatisfaction of some, and the resignation of others; make the dissatisfied children appear ridiculous, for this is an opportunity to make humor and satire teach a lesson.

*c.* Introduce an adult to reprove the dissatisfied children; ask rhetorical questions, as whether the class would desire ever to merit such reproof.

*d.* Think aloud, betraying your own attitude towards the rain.

*e.* Allow the adult in the story to analyze the imaginary thoughts of the raindrop; this leads directly to the description as contained in the "Religion Hour" reader.

*f.* After these thoughts are portrayed, rhetorical questions should be put as to the meritorious character of the raindrop's obedience, and the willingness of the class to obey in like manner; the teacher should not fail to betray artfully her own willingness to follow the example of the raindrop.

## Dramatization.

*A boy or girl takes the character of the raindrop; others in convenient numbers play the part of companion raindrops. They continuously chase each other about in the background, while the leading character flits lightly back and forward in the foreground.*

RAINDROP: Do you know who I am?

COMPANIONS: Yes, we know; you are like us, you are a drop of rain.

RAINDROP: Do you know where I live?

COMPANIONS: You live with us, away up above the houses.

RAINDROP: And high above the trees.

COMPANIONS: Yes, high above the trees.

RAINDROP: *(bends forward and looks downward)* I see boys and girls playing.

COMPANIONS: So do we.

RAINDROP: I shall go down to play with them when God asks me to go.

COMPANIONS: And so shall we.

RAINDROP: I shall go because God the Son left His home.

COMPANIONS: For boys and girls.

RAINDROP: To make them happy.

COMPANIONS: God is telling you now that you must go.

RAINDROP: Farewell, I must do what He says. I must go. *(Exits R.)*

**Silent Reading.** *Bricks for a Building.*

The story is the building. The answers to questions written on the blackboard are the bricks that the children are supposed to supply. This exercise should take place after the story in the "Religion Hour" reader has been read in class. The books are closed. The reading exercise consists in reading the written questions on the blackboard.

Divide class into two groups. Have consecutive members of the groups read and answer the succeeding questions, alternating from one group to the other. He who can not supply a brick is counted out. At the end, the group with the greater number of survivors is adjudged the winner.

Appropriate questions for this story are:

Where is the home of the drop of rain?

Is the home of the drop of rain above you?

Is the home of the drop of rain above the trees?

Are the trees above the home of the drop of rain?

Is the home of the drop of rain near the trees?

Does the drop of rain look down from its home?

What does the drop of rain see?

What does the drop of rain see the boys and girls doing?

Does the drop of rain like to see boys and girls playing?

Would the drop of rain like the boys and girls to come to its home?

Will the boys and girls go to the home of the drop of rain?

Will the drop of rain come to the home of the boys and girls?

Will the drop of rain do what God wants?

Why will the drop of rain do what God wants?

### Related Stories from Other Sources.

Christ calls James and John to leave their father, Zebedee, and to follow Him. They obey. (St. Matthew, iv, 22).

St. Francis Xavier (December 3) left all his friends to labor in India, Malacca, Japan, and China, dying in the East. It is related that in making his journey to the East, he was within easy reach of his parents' home, but refused to visit them lest he be deterred from his purpose.

Paul Revere accepting the dangerous mission of notifying the Minute Men of the march of the British to Concord. He had no security that he would ever see his relatives again.

Lafayette, leaving his home in France to help the colonists win their independence.

"The Oak and the Reed" (Aesop's Fables). In this story the oak will not yield to the superior power of the storm and is uprooted, while the reeds that bend willingly remain unharmed by it.

"The Cloud" ("Stories to Tell Children," Bryant). Here the surrender of life by the cloud to help men is portrayed.

### GOD'S HOUSE (8)

Michael is a good boy. He likes to do what God wants. God sees Michael all day long. God sees all boys and girls. God sees Michael doing good. Michael likes to go to God's house. He knows that God the Son is there. When Michael can not go in, he takes off his cap as he goes by. One day Frank saw Michael do this. Frank did not know who is in God's house. He said that Michael took off his cap to a house. Michael told Frank that God the Son is in that house. After that, Frank also took off his cap to God.

### Related Stories in "Teacher Tells a Story."

This story should be preceded by story 7, and followed by story 9. Other stories of similar thought matter are stories 135 and 145.

### Development of "God's House."

*a.* Establish interest contact by reference to parish church, having children look out the window to see it, if possible; think aloud, pondering upon the reason for the building of the church; say that you will have to go to the class for information.

*b.* To stimulate thought, ask the children if they know why the church was built, but do not permit an answer until after the story is told. If any child seems to insist upon answering bethink yourself immediately of the story; say that you heard about a little boy who seemed to know why churches are built; and that you will tell them what he did, so they may know, too.

*c.* Preface your story by telling how you know that Michael is a good boy, stressing honesty of character, and the performance of his duty, whether his superiors were watching or not. Assign the cause for this, his knowledge that God is watching all. Give an example, for instance, of companions coaxing him to disobey, introducing some humor in their ridiculing him, but show him firm in his obedience.

d. Show this same firmness acting in his loyalty to Christ in the tabernacle. Describe Frank as an irreligious boy, ignorant of Catholic teaching, but willing to ridicule Catholic practice. Say that Michael knew all this. Show the struggle that went on in Michael's mind when he was tempted at the thought of Frank's ridicule to forego tipping his cap. Picture counter representations by his guardian angel and by the devil; this will make the tipping of his cap a victory, and a dramatic one. Think aloud and say that you would be glad to please God as Michael did in his victory. Ask rhetorically, if the children do not wish so, too.

e. Show Michael's defense of his faith, but his distrust of himself in the beginning. Say that Frank's determination to take off his cap, also, should show that even children can do God's work, and that they ought not distrust their ability. Think aloud and say that if you were a child you would never be afraid to explain what you knew about Our Lord, and that you hope your class will not be afraid, either.

## Dramatization.

*Two boys play the roles.*

*Scene I. Street in front of church. (Michael exits from imaginary church.)*

MICHAEL: I have just come from God's house. I like to go to God's house. (*Looks upward.*) God sees me doing it. He sees me doing every thing I do. He likes me to go to His house, because God the Son is there. (*Walks R. towards exit.*) I wish all boys and girls would go to God's house, too. (*Exit R.*)

*Scene II. Same. Michael enter from L.*

MICHAEL: I must hurry, I can not go into God's house now. But I will tip my cap and tell Him I love Him. *(Enter Frank from R.)* There's Frank. I know he will make fun of me. I wish he would turn his back. I am getting nearer God's house, too. I must not pass without tipping my cap. No! I will not pass without tipping it. *(Tips his cap, while Frank bursts out into laughter.)*

FRANK: That's the best I ever saw! Ho! ho! ho! tipping your cap to a house! Ho! Ho! Ho! *(Michael is going to pass him without answering back; but Frank gets in his way, and pushes him lightly but tauntingly).* Did you hear what I said? Tipping your cap to an old house. Ho! ho! ho! *(Michael faces Frank defiantly).*

MICHAEL: Is that so? That's all you know about it. I wasn't tipping my cap just to an old house.

FRANK: Well, I don't see anything else but a house around here.

MICHAEL: But this is God's house. I was tipping my cap to God the Son. He lives there.

FRANK: *(becoming solemn)* Does God really live there?

MICHAEL: Yes, He is there to help us. He died long ago on the cross to save us. But He came back to His boys and girls again.

FRANK: I did not know that.

MICHAEL: Don't you think that I should tip my cap to God for doing that?

FRANK: Yes, and I am going to do it, too. *(Frank and Michael both go to C., tip their caps, and exeunt, Michael R., Frank L.)*

**Silent Reading.** *Answer Search.*

This exercise should take place before the story in the "Religion Hour" reader has been read in class.

Divide the class into two groups. Tell the pupils you are going to ask some questions, one at a time, some of which have more than one answer. Ask them to find all the answers to the questions they can, checking the places in the book, if necessary, to help their memories. The child who finds the correct number of answers first scores a point for his side. If none finds the maximum number, the child who had the greatest number of answers first, scores.

Sample questions:

> What does God see? (Three answers.)
> What did Frank do? (Three answers.)
> What did Michael like to do? (Two answers.)
> What did Michael tell Frank? (One answer.)

The purpose of this exercise is to train the children to read quickly through a passage, with the purpose of their search in the foreground of their minds.

### Related Stories from Other Sources.

God commanded that the Israelites should keep purest olive oil burning before the Holy of Holies, where the Ark of the Covenant, the type of the Real Presence, was preserved. (Exodus, xxvii, 20–21.)

Our Lord drove the money changers from the Temple. (St. Matthew, xxi, 12–13.)

Michael's defense of the faith exemplified in higher degree by St. Peter Canisius, who was Apostolic Nuncio to Council of Trent, and who revived the zeal of Christian princes, reformed the universities, brought back whole cities to the Faith, and defended the Faith in public conferences against the attacks of heretics in Germany, Austria, Poland, and Bohemia. (June 25).

St. Norbert (June 6) defended the Blessed Sacrament against the heretic, Tankelin, in Antwerp. On another occasion, when apostates had buried the Blessed Sacrament in filthy places because of their hatred, he sought until he found all the Sacred Hosts, uninjured, and brought them back to the tabernacle.

St. Tarcisius (October 7) was a young cleric who was entrusted with carrying the Blessed Sacrament to the Christians in prison. A pagan mob attacked him, and killed him in their attempt to get hold of the Blessed Sacrament. When they searched his clothing, they found that It had miraculously disappeared.

Blessed Thomas More had a high political position in England under Henry VIII. When the latter rebelled against the Church, Blessed Thomas resigned his office, and later suffered martyrdom for his loyalty to the Faith.

"The Lamb and the Wolf" (Aesop's Fables). In this story a lamb fled for refuge to the temple. The wolf cried out to him that the priest would slay him in sacrifice. The lamb replied that it would be better for him to die in sacrifice than to be eaten by the wolf.

## THE CROSS ON THE LOCKET (13)

Rose loves her father. Her father is good to her. He wants Rose to love God. He tells her about God the Son. Rose knows that God the Son was put on a cross. She knows that He was put there for us. Her father knew that Rose loves God the Son. So he gave her a locket. It had a cross on it. After that, Rose loved her father more than ever. She put the locket on one day before her friends. One little girl friend was bad. She made fun of the cross. Rose said she put it on to thank God. She said many good things about God the Son. Then the bad girl also wanted to have a locket with a cross.

**Related Stories in "Teacher Tells a Story."**

This story should be preceded by stories 10–12, inclusive; and followed by story 14. Other stories of similar thought matter are: 60–63, inclusive.

**Development of "The Cross on the Locket."**

*a.* Create interest by singling out some child that is wearing a locket in the class-room; if there is no locket, look for some piece of jewelry, a bracelet or a ring, for example; if you can single out a piece with religious symbolism, so much the better.

*b.* Interpret the motive of the child in wearing it as a desire to look pretty in God's eyes. Show how religious emblems do this more certainly than merely secular ornaments.

*c.* Think aloud, telling what kind of jewelry you would wear, if you were to have any. Say, if it is true, that you deprive yourself of jewelry so as to be sure you will not "show off." If you wear a ring, talk to yourself audibly about the reason for it.

*d.* Ask rhetorical questions about the motives the children would have in wearing ornaments.

*e.* Say that you heard of a little girl who made another love God by explaining her motive in wearing a locket.

*f.* Praise the love existing between Rose and her father. Say that you think all the children in your class love their parents. Ask rhetorically how many children love God the Son. Thinking aloud, ask yourself why they should love Him; be sure to answer this question with emphasis upon the degradation He suffered for them. Introduce some humor into the ridicule of the bad little girl, but be careful not to direct it against the cross, but against the motives of Rose in wearing the locket. Question yourself whether the children in class would be courageous enough to answer as Rose did. Assure yourself aloud that all would be. Ask rhetorically if the children do not think that God loved Rose more after her instruction, than He did before. Ask again if they are not going to imitate Rose, when opportunity offers.

## Dramatization.

*(Enter Rose and First Companion, R.)*

ROSE: My father loves God very much.

FIRST COMPANION: So does mine.

ROSE: Does he tell you about God the Son?

FIRST COMPANION: Yes, he tells me about His death.

ROSE: Don't you love God the Son for dying for you?

FIRST COMPANION: Indeed, I do.

*(Enter Second Companion L.)*

SECOND COMPANION: Hello, girls, won't you come and play school?

ROSE: Yes, I like to play school.

SECOND COMPANION: Oh! what is that you have on?

*(Points to locket.)*

ROSE: Why, that's a gold cross.

SECOND COMPANION: Oh! you want to look holy, don't you?

FIRST COMPANION: I think that's unkind.

SECOND COMPANION: The first thing we know, we'll be playing Sunday school.

FIRST COMPANION: I would be glad to play Sunday school.

SECOND COMPANION: Why don't you wear a star, or a heart, instead of a cross?

ROSE: I will tell you why. Because God the Son died on a cross for you and me. I do not wear this just to look holy, but to thank God the Son.

SECOND COMPANION: Why did He die for us?

ROSE: So that we could go to Heaven.

SECOND COMPANION: Can I go, too?

ROSE: Yes, if you love Him and thank Him.

SECOND COMPANION: Well, I am going to do that. I am going to thank Him as you are, by wearing a locket with a cross on it. And now, I am willing to play Sunday school, too, if you want.

*(Exeunt three L.)*

**Silent Reading.** *Fallen Stars.*

After reading the story in class, divide the class into two groups. Tell them that during the night a number of stars fell into the story they have read, and you want the children to find how many of each kind are there. Various words to be found will be the stars, and the number of times they occur will be the number of stars of that kind in the story. The words should be given one at a time; the child who first finds correctly the number of times the given word occurs scores a point for his side. The purpose of this exercise is to give facility in recognizing the same word in different contexts.

Appropriate words for this exercise are, with the number of times each occurs:

her—8, Rose,—6, God—6, the—6, she—5, Son—4, he—4, cross—4, put—4, it—3, that—4, locket—3, said—2.

**Related Stories from Other Sources.**

Moses erected a brazen serpent on a cross to cure the Israelites of the fatal illness caused by the plague of serpents. This cross is a type of Calvary. (Numbers, xxi, 6-9.)

St. Peter, martyred under Nero, loved the cross to the extent of dying upon it, head downward, out of humility.

St. Joseph of Leonissa (February 4) spent entire nights before the crucifix. In undergoing an operation, he held a crucifix before him, to remember the suffering of Christ, and bore the pain without a murmur.

St. Helen, mother of Constantine, made a pilgrimage to Jerusalem to discover the cross on which Christ died. Three crosses were found on Mount Calvary; each was applied to a woman incurably afflicted. The third, the true cross, healed her. St. Helen built a church on Mount Calvary in which the cross might be preserved (May 3).

Constantine, her son, in striving to gain the emperor's throne, was engaged in battle at the Milvian Bridge, when he saw a cross in the sky, with the words, "Through this sign thou shalt conquer." He made a standard in the form of a cross, and gained a complete victory.

The gratitude of Rose may be emphasized by the fable of ingratitude contained in "The Farmer and the Snake" (Aesop's Fables). The farmer found a snake almost frozen to death, and placed it in his bosom to bring it back to life. When the stiffness of cold had gone, the snake repaid the kindness by injecting its poison into the farmer's breast.

## A Helping Hand (17 and 18)

Terry is a very little boy. But he is very kind. When Terry went to school to-day, he saw an old woman. She looked very sad. Near her was a big basket. It was filled with things to eat. The old woman could not take another step with it. She told that to Terry. Terry is not very strong, but he said he would help the old woman. With Terry's help she got the basket home. The old woman was the mother of Father Connors. And Father Connors was glad that Terry had been so kind. He thanked Terry by saying a Mass for him.

### Related Stories in "Teacher Tells a Story."

This story should be preceded by stories 15-17, inclusive, and followed by stories 19-23, inclusive. Other stories of similar thought matter are 54-56, inclusive.

### Development of "A Helping Hand."

*a.* Create interest by speaking of the parish priest's mother, if the children are acquainted with her. If not, choose some pious old woman whom they have likely met as she came from morning Mass. If there is none such, ask the children if any of them has his grandmother living with him; have such a child tell some of the things his grandmother does to help about the house.

*b.* Think aloud, bringing out the loveableness of old people, and your desire to be of service to them.

*c.* Ask rhetorical questions, as whether the children are not anxious also to help the old.

*d.* Introduce some humor by picturing various members of the class in their old age; become serious again by saying that in their old age God will repay them if they, while young, have been good to the old.

*e.* Say you know that God will reward Terry for his kind act; tell the story of "A Helping Hand"; make the old woman appear ready to give up in despair her attempt to get the basket home; show that Terry is tempted to pass on without helping; introduce various pretexts that suggest themselves to his mind; show that he conquers the temptation.

*f.* Room for pathos is to be found in the conversation that you will invent for Terry and the old woman; have her shed a tear of joy because of Terry's kindness; make him misunderstand the tear, and assure her that she need have no fear because of his great strength; explain the misunderstanding to the children; call attention to Terry's confidence in himself.

*g.* When Father Connors meets Terry have him feel Terry's biceps, whistle a little, and shake his head as one convinced; say that Terry threw out his chest just a little at that; make Terry grateful for Father Connors' return service in the Holy Sacrifice.

**Dramatization.**

*Two boys and a girl play the characters of Terry, Father Connors, and the latter's mother, respectively.*

*Scene I. (Enter R. the old woman, carrying in over-burdened fashion a large basket. She walks C. and puts basket down, sighs and attempts painfully to stand erect).*

OLD WOMAN: I should not have bought so many things. The basket is too heavy. *(Sighs again).* I do not think I can move it another step. *(Looks off L.)* If I had the help of one of those boys playing ball there, I might be able to get it home. *(Shakes head in despair).* But I shall never be able to carry it that far.

*(Enter Terry running L; stops short when he sees the old woman.)*

TERRY *(thinking aloud):* I can't wait to help her. I must go to the store for mother. *(Runs past old woman, but halts a step or two beyond her).* But Father Connors says we must be kind to the old. *(Shrugs shoulders).* But I have no time today. *(Runs off R.)*

OLD WOMAN *(looking off R. and shaking head in disappointment):* And he looked like a kind boy! *(She takes out her handkerchief and cries).*

TERRY *(running in from R. and up to the old woman):* I will help you. I must go to the store, but I'll help you first.

OLD WOMAN: Are you sure you are strong enough?

TERRY *(rolling up his sleeve and showing his muscle):* Strong? Look at that! *(The old woman dries her eyes.)* Don't cry, we shall get this basket to your home in no time. *(They take hold of the basket and exeunt L.)*

*Scene II. (Enter Father Connors L.)*

FATHER CONNORS: I am glad to get home to see mother. A visit does both of us much good.

*(Terry runs in R. and without looking up bumps into Father Connors.)*

FATHER CONNORS: Here, here, young man, look where you are going! *(He recognizes Terry)* Why, Terry, what are you doing here? *(Enter the old woman R.)*

OLD WOMAN: I'll tell you what he was doing. He helped me home with my heavy basket, when I thought I would never get it here.

FATHER CONNORS: Did you do that for my mother, Terry? You must be a strong man. *(Feels Terry's biceps, whistles quietly.)* Yes, sir, it's true. I never thought you were so strong, Terry. *(Father C. thinks aloud):* Now, what can I do in return?

TERRY *(running off L.):* I don't want anything, Father. Only pray for me.

FATHER CONNORS: I will, Terry; I will say my Mass for you tomorrow. *(Turning to his mother)* And now, mother, you must come into the house and tell me all about it.

*(Exeunt both R.)*

**Silent Reading.** *Race Horses.*

Before the story is read in class, divide the class into two groups; tell them that they are all to be race horses; and that they are to run as fast in their minds as they can. They are to commence at the beginning of the story and read as fast as possible until the teacher calls, "Time." They mark the place where they finished, and count the number of words read. He who has read the greatest number of words is then questioned on the subject matter. If he answers satisfactorily, he scores a point for his side. The exercise may be continued until the story has been covered in this way. A minute should be ample time for the reading of approximately three sentences. The purpose of this exercise is to develop speed with exactness in reading.

**Related Stories from Other Sources.**

The Good Samaritan found the man who had been robbed and injured by thieves, and whom the priest and the levite had passed by. The Good Samaritan administered first aid, and took him to a hospital, where he told those in charge to spare no cost, for he would be responsible for the expenses involved in bringing the injured man back to health. (St. Luke, x, 30–37.)

St. Martin, Bishop of Tours, while a catechumen and a soldier, divided his cloak in order to warm a naked beggar (November 11).

Father Damien, a missionary in the Hawaiian Islands, volunteered to serve the lepers. He administered to them spiritually and temporally, and fifteen years after he had volunteered, years spent with the lepers, he himself died of that disease.

Florence Nightingale labored in the Crimea during

the Crimean War, to make the nursing of the sick and wounded soldiers more efficient. As a result of her labors, her own health was permanently impaired.

"The Wind and the Sun" (Aesop's Fables) shows the contrast between harshness and kindness. The wind tried to make a man take off his coat by blowing fiercely; but the man only buttoned his coat more tightly about him. The sun gave him of its warmth, and he took his coat off.

"The Wheat-Field" (in "Golden Windows," by Richards) shows how a toiler in the wheat-field came home with no sheaves to show for his labor; but it tells that he was admitted to his reward because he had helped others throughout the day.

### THE TOY SOLDIERS (24)

Mr. Jones gives his son, Robert, things to play with. He also gives his little girl, Ruth, things to play with. One day Robert was not home. Ruth wanted to play. There was no one to play with. She took Robert's toy soldiers. She put them all over the table. They were not in line, as they should be. Robert came in, and saw Ruth playing. He did not like the way she had put the soldiers on the table. He put them in lines, not too close to each other. Ruth said they looked much better that way. We are all soldiers. God puts us in line. We get out of line when we are bad. That makes God feel sad.

### Related Stories in "Teacher Tells a Story."

This story should be preceded by stories 25–35, inclusive. Other stories of similar thought matter are: 52–55, inclusive.

### Development of "The Toy Soldiers."

*a.* Discover whether any of the children have toy soldiers; if possible, have one of them tell about his own; if none have toy soldiers, think aloud yourself and tell of a trip through a toy shop at Christmas time. Tell how you stopped to admire the soldierly bearing of these tin toys, and how you were tempted to buy a set for the children of your class.

*b.* Say that Mr. Jones must have been in the same shop, for he gave a present of toy soldiers to his little boy, Robert.

*c.* Go on with the story of "The Toy Soldiers," spending much emphasis on the ludicrous appearance of the army as arranged by Ruth. There is a great opportunity for humor here. Say, for instance, one of the soldiers seemed to be keeping more than the right distance from another, as though the other wanted to step on his feet; say, again, that one was so close to another that it seemed as though he had a secret to tell him that the rest were not to hear.

*d.* Make Robert enjoy the scene; emphasize the care and precision he uses to place the soldiers correctly. Think aloud and say that God used greater care in placing boys and girls in their positions.

*e.* Ask rhetorical questions whether the children want to look foolish by being out of line, or whether they are going to keep the positions God gave them.

**Dramatization.**

*A boy and a girl play the characters. (Enter Robert and Ruth, R. E.).*

ROBERT: You see that soldiers must be in line to look well, don't you?

RUTH: I do now, but they looked all right the way I had them before I saw them them in line.

ROBERT: But they would not look all right to you now, would they?

RUTH : No, because I know how they ought to stand, now.

ROBERT : So you would not put them out of line, again; nor too close to each other?

RUTH : No, I would put them in line as you did.

ROBERT : Ruth, did you ever know that we are soldiers?

RUTH : Why no! Are we?

ROBERT : Yes, we are. God places us in line, and not too close to each other.

RUTH : So God knows how we ought to stand.

ROBERT : Yes, and He is hurt when we get out of line.

RUTH : How do we get out of line?

ROBERT : By being bad.

RUTH : I will not be bad, then. Will you?

ROBERT : I will not, either, I do not want God to feel sad.

**Silent Reading.** *Missing Word Game.*

After reading the story in class, divide the class into two groups. Books are to be closed. Write on the blackboard the first sentence as it stands in the "Religion Hour" reader, leaving a blank space for one of the words of the sentence. The child that finds the word from memory first scores for his side. Then take up the second sentence in like manner, and so on to the end. The purpose of this exercise is to drill the children in associating sentences nearly similar, but slightly distinct from each other. It is an aid to preciseness.

**Related Stories from Other Sources.**

Lot's wife did not obey orders, did not keep in line with her husband, but stopped to look back at the destruction of Sodom and Gomorrah, and was turned into a pillar of salt (Genesis, xix, 26).

St. Joan of Arc was a poor peasant girl. None would have thought that God intended her for a general of an army. But that was just her vocation. She was true to it, and instilled the same spirit into the French army. She prevented the French crown from being placed on the head of the English king. She succeeded where men had failed before her. After the French prince was crowned, her work was done. She wanted to return home. But the newly crowned French king would *not let her go*. But now she was out of line. Instead of being successful she began to fail. At last she became the prisoner of the English, and was burned to death by them (May 30).

Benjamin Franklin had a schedule of duties for each day. He knew that it was only by keeping each one in its place, that he could keep himself in line, i. e., that he would be faithful to them all.

"The Monkey and the Camel" (Aesop's Fables) tells how the camel tried to dance like the monkey in order to win applause as the monkey had. He was so awkward that he received nothing but abuse. He was out of line.

"The Prominent Man" (in "Golden Windows," by Richards) shows how a man thought to be of great consequence to his neighbors, may prove upon occasion a hindrance to them. He can be out of line.

## THE FOOLISH BEAR (37)

A little bear was looking for a home. One day he saw a wolf coming after him. "What are you doing?" asked the wolf. "I am looking for a home," said the bear. "You do not need a home. Come and live with me," said the wolf. "But you would eat me. My mother said so." "What does she know? She does not like me, that's all." The bear went to the home of the wolf. But he would not go to bed. When the wolf saw this, he tried to eat him. But the bear ran away as fast as he could. He was hurt when the wolf bit him. But he was glad he did not go to bed in the wolf's house. His mother was right, after all.

### Related Stories in "Teacher Tells a Story."

This story should be followed by story 38. Stories of similar thought matter are: 48-51, inclusive.

### Development of "The Foolish Bear."

*a.* Create interest by having one of the children tell what he thinks of the bear he saw at the zoo. If this can not be done, think aloud and describe the bear you saw. Contrast the strength and size of the adult bear with that of the cub.

*b.* Inject a little humor by discussing the taste of the wolf. Say that he is indifferent whether his food is cooked or not, or whether it is properly seasoned, or whether the proper table implements are at hand. Tell them that this is especially true when the tender meat of the cub bear is in sight.

*c.* Note that the mother bears know that, because they have lived long enough to hear of many cub bears who served the wolf by being his food.

*d.* Think aloud and remark that cub bears should respect the knowledge that years bring to their mothers.

*e.* Show the folly of the inexperienced cub in distrusting his mother who had previously been kind to him, to accept the word of a perfect stranger, whom he had reason to believe was his enemy. Ask rhetorically whether the children do not think the cub very ungrateful to his mother. Think aloud and say that it would have served him right, if the wolf had eaten him.

*f.* Do not fail to show that the cub's vigilance, such as it was, was due to his mother's warning. Attribute his escape to the kindness of his mother. Think aloud and say you hope the little bear thought of that, and heeded her advice more willingly after that.

## Dramatization.

*Have two boys take the characters of huntsmen, with improvised guns. (Enter both R. E.)*

FIRST HUNTSMAN: *(looking off L.)* It is a wolf.

SECOND HUNTSMAN: *(lifting gun to shoulder)* It's an easy shot.

FIRST H.: *(grasps the other's arm)* Do not shoot! There is a little bear with him. Let us see what they will do.

SECOND H.: *(lowers gun)* They are going towards that hole in the hill.

FIRST H.: Yes, that's the wolf's home.

SECOND H.: The bear will never come out alive.

FIRST H.: I hope he does not go into the wolf's home.

SECOND H.: *(raises gun again)* I am going to save the bear. *(Shoots).* Too late! They have gone into the wolf's home.

*(Pantomime for two or three minutes; the boys go about aiming their guns in the air, shooting, picking up the birds they have killed, and placing them on an imaginary pile).*

FIRST H.: *(looking suddenly off L.)* There, there he goes. He's not killed after all.

SECOND H.: No, the bear's safe, but there's the wolf right after him.

FIRST H.: We must help the bear. *(Raises gun and shoots)*. Well, the wolf's dead this time.

SECOND H.: And the bear is safe.

FIRST H.: Yes, but it was I who saved him.

*(Each takes up part of the imaginary load of game, puts it on his shoulder, and both exeunt R. E.)*

## Silent Reading. *Cross Questioning.*

Before reading the story in class, divide the class into two groups. Have all the pupils read the story, or part of the story, to themselves. Then have each group stand in line facing the other. The pupils of the two groups alternate in asking questions of the group opposite. The questions must pertain to the story matter. If the questioning lags, the teacher may ask questions of the groups alternately. As a child fails to answer he takes his seat. The group that has the greater number standing when the questioning comes to an end is counted the winner.

## Related Stories from Other Sources.

Roboam, the son of Solomon, listened to evil counsellors to his own loss (III Kings, xii, 8-19).

St. Anastasius was a Persian soldier who had come to a knowledge of Christianity through his service in Palestine. After his conversion he was thrown into prison. Every effort was made to induce him to renounce Christianity. He was offered a high dignity in the Persian court, if he would cease to profess Christ. He was constant, however, and died a martyr's death (January 22).

St. Symphorian was tempted in like manner by the promise of riches and honor to give up Christianity.

He rejected all the offers, and died by the sword (August 22).

Benedict Arnold listened to the temptation to be a traitor to his country. He escaped death, but lived in misery, despised by men for his treachery.

"The Sick Stag" (Aesop's Fables) visited by selfish friends was deprived of his food, because they ate it for him. A good example of the destructive power of evil companionship.

"The Cat and the Mice" (Aesop's Fables) shows the vigilance of the mice who would not be led within striking distance of the cat, even though she hung herself on a hook to appear like a meal-bag, and thus deceive them.

"The Wolf and the Sheep" (Aesop's Fables) sets forth the prudence of the sheep who, when asked by a wounded wolf to bring him some water, refused on the score that if he brought the drink he would have to supply the meat also.

### THE GREEDY MOUSE (39)

Teeny and Tiny were two little mice. Their mother told them not to want too much to eat. One day their mother said they could go to town. They found a home in the town. There were many little boys and girls in that home. One day they had good things to eat. Tiny also wanted to have some good things to eat. So he went into the room where the boys and girls were eating. Tiny would not do as his mother told him. Soon one of the little girls saw Tiny. Her father ran after Tiny and hit him on the back. Tiny got away. But his back was very sore. Teeny was not hurt. He did as his mother told him.

## Related Stories in "Teacher Tells a Story."

This story should be followed by story 40.

## Development of "The Greedy Mouse."

*a.* Arouse interest by asking one of the children to tell of his experiences with a mouse.

*b.* Introduce some humor by describing some of the antics of people frightened by mice.

*c.* Show that mice are disliked by men because of the destruction they cause; think aloud and say that children who destroy things can not be loved by their friends.

*d.* Say that you heard of a little mouse who did not know how much people disliked him. Tell how the mother mouse warned this mouse, Tiny, and his brother, Teeny, not to be greedy.

*e.* Tell something about the children in the home; interest can be developed by describing their toys or their manner of dress.

*f.* Make the most of the party that was held; speak of the games the children played before dinner; tell about the table decorations; introduce some humor by describing comic favors set at the places of each child.

*g.* Make the discovery of Tiny dramatic. Picture the joy of the children at the table, thinking nothing about the mouse. Have Tiny advance a step, then run back at the sudden movement of a chair; make him advance a little farther on each successive attempt until finally he is under the table where all the crumbs are; have him gradually forget where he is, and finally brush against the shoe of one of the children. The child looks down and screams; Tiny is paralyzed for a second, then begins to run; the child's father throws a spoon at Tiny, who escapes, but with injury.

*h.* Think aloud and commend the obedience of Teeny.

## Dramatization.

*Have six children play the roles of boys and girls; a boy for the father of the house, and a girl for the mother. Seat them about a table, real or imaginary, mother and father at the ends.*

MOTHER: We are glad to have all of you here today.

FATHER: Yes, we want you to have a good time. This is our little girl's birthday, you know.

FIRST CHILD: I am having a very good time.

SECOND CHILD: And so am I.

THIRD CHILD: I shall never forget the fun we had playing games.

MOTHER: *(lifting imaginary plate of cake)* Pass this plate of cake around. I think all you children can eat a second piece.

*(Pantomime, plate goes around table, each child takes a piece).*

FATHER: And after you have eaten the cake, there is a big box of candy waiting here for you.

MOTHER: I think they should have another glass of lemonade. This will be only the second. *(She lifts imaginary pitcher and pours into imaginary glasses, passed to her by all the children).*

*(The little girl of the house at this moment becomes uneasy; she looks down; she screams; she points R.; the father looks R.; seizes imaginary spoon, and throws at floor in that direction).*

FATHER: He got away that time; but he will not come back again. *(All are seated; pantomime of eating cake and drinking lemonade).*

FATHER: *(after they have all put down their glasses and folded imaginary napkins)* Now, we shall go out on the porch; we can bring the candy out there, and have a good time playing games for it.

*(Exeunt all L.)*

**Silent Reading.** *Acting Your Name.*

Before reading the story in class, assign all words in a given sentence to different pupils, changing the order in which you assign them from the order of their occurrence in the sentence. Then have all the children read that sentence. Children to whom words in that sentence have been assigned (whose names are in it) are asked to come to the front of the room, and to arrange themselves in the order in which their names appear in the sentence. The children may be allowed to consult the book as often as need be, provided no oral reading of the sentence is permitted. The purpose of this exercise is to introduce the child to the importance which order of words plays in expressing ideas.

To illustrate this exercise let us take the first sentence. Seven children are given the names of the words in it. After it is read silently, the seven children are asked to come to the front of the room. The child named, "Teeny" should take his place at the head of the line; he who is named, "and," the second place, and so on. If any child cannot find his place, any other in the seats may take it, after raising his hand, and asking permission to take the place of "Teeny," or of "and," or of some other of the words. Or the teacher may ask who wants to take place of that word, checking the child who responds by asking what word is missing.

The teachers should not use sentences 2, 7, 8; there is a repetition of the same word in these sentences. This may cause confusion.

**Related Stories from Other Sources.**

Eleazar abstained from eating the meat that was offered him, even though it was not pork, because the impression would be given to younger people that he had eaten pork, and they would be tempted to weakness through his bad example. He was put to death as a result (II Macchabees vi, 18–31).

St. Anthony (January 17) had only bread and water for food; he would take that only after sunset, and some days he would abstain from it entirely.

The Hessian troops in the British army through intemperance were unprepared when Washington, after crossing the Delaware, assaulted them at Trenton.

"The Dog and His Shadow" (Aesop's Fables) shows how a dog seeing himself reflected in the water, tried to snatch the food from the imaginary dog's mouth, and so lost that which he was carrying in his own.

"The Hen and the Golden Eggs" (Aesop's Fables) tells how a farmer and his wife thinking that their hen laid a golden egg each day because she had a lump of gold inside, killed her, only to find that she differed in no way from other hens.

## THE BLACK CHICK (46)

There was one time a white hen. She had nine white chicks. She had also one black chick. She loved the white chicks. She loved the black one, too. But the white chicks did not love the black one. Sometimes they tried to hurt it. But the mother hen always took it under her wing. The white chicks could not hurt it, there. The mother hen was sad when she saw how bad the white chicks were. She wanted them to love the black chick. God is our Father. He loves white boys and girls. But He loves black boys and girls, too. He wants white boys and girls to love those who are black.

## Related Stories in "Teacher Tells a Story."

*This story should be followed by story 47.*

### Development of "The Black Chick."

*a.* Ask the children if they have ever seen a hen with her brood of chicks. Have one of them tell how carefully the mother watches the chicks. Ask them if they think there is any difference between white feathers and black. Tell them that you knew of some little chicks who thought so.

*b.* Think aloud and say that perhaps you should first tell where the chicks came from. Describe the mother hen patiently setting on the nest waiting for the hatching of ten white eggs. Think aloud and suggest that a mother who spent so much time and care on the eggs would surely love the little chicks that came from them. Describe her delight when she heard the scratching inside the eggs. Show how joyful she was when the chicks finally broke through. An opportunity for humorous allusions suggests itself here; for instance, you might say that the mother hen would have clapped her hands, if she had them, but she did the next best thing and tried to clap her wings.

*c.* Speak very solemnly and show how this joyful family was thrown into sadness; the first sign the mother hen notes is when one of her white chicks pecks at the one black chick; from that time on, one white chick after another showed his dislike for the black chick. Say how hurt the mother hen felt; remark that the white chicks hated the chick their mother loved. Ask rhetorically if all the chicks did not come from white eggs. Ask yourself aloud why they should hate the black chick.

*d.* Ask yourself aloud if you hate black chicks; answer that you love them just as much as you do the white ones. Ask yourself whether you love black boys and girls as you do white; answer affirmatively that you do.  Say to yourself that God made them and loves them, and that you can not hate them without hurting God.

*e.* Ask the children, finally, whether they are going to act like the white chicks, or whether they are going to love all whom God loves.

**Dramatization.**

A boy and a girl act the characters.

BOY: *(looking off R.)*  What a nice white hen.

GIRL: *(also looking off R.)*  And see the little chicks, too.

BOY: How many are there?

GIRL: Let me see: one, two, three, five, six, and three over there *(points)* are nine.

BOY: Did you count the black one?

GIRL: No, where is it?

BOY: *(pointing)* There.

GIRL: That makes ten.

BOY: Look, how kind the mother hen is.

GIRL: Yes, she has just given them a worm to eat.

BOY: *(excited)* Look, the white ones are trying to keep the black one away.

GIRL: They are running after it.  Oh! run and save it.  They might kill it.

BOY: *(commences to run)* They will not kill it.  I will save it.  *(Stops after a few steps).*  The mother has taken it under her wing; she has saved it.

GIRL: Yes, she loves the black chick, too.  But come, we must give her some corn for being so kind.
                    *(Exit both R.)*

**Silent Reading.**  *Foreign Word Game.*

Before reading the story divide the class into two groups.  Take each sentence separately and, changing the order, write the words of that sentence on the blackboard, adding one word that is not in the sentence in the book. Children open their books and read to discover which word on the blackboard is the foreign word. He who first answers correctly scores a point for his side. The purpose of this exercise is to teach economy of words, to show that a certain number of words suffice to express a given thought, and that others are superfluous.

**Related Stories from Other Sources.**

St. Paul, the Apostle, recognized no distinction of race in his apostleship (Epistle to the Romans, i, 13–15, I Epistle to the Corinthians, ix, 19–23).

St. Peter Claver (September 9), a Spanish Jesuit, was sent to Cartagena, the great slave-market of the West Indies. There for forty years he labored as apostle, father, physician, and friend of the slaves (negroes).

St. Francis Solano (July 24), a Franciscan, on his way to preach the Gospel in South America, was involved in a wreck at sea. In the midst of the danger his attention was given to instructing and baptizing the negroes on board, many of whom perished soon afterwards through the sinking of the vessel.

Abraham Lincoln will always stand out as the champion of the negro. In his campaign for President his attitude was unmistakable. It led to the secession of the Confederacy upon his election. The Emancipation Proclamation, though a war measure, embodied the sincere sentiments of Lincoln.

"The Brother and Sister" (Aesop's Fables) shows that beauty of soul in their children is loved by parents more than beauty of body.

"The Fox and the Leopard" (Aesop's Fables)

teaches that the shrewdness of mind of the fox is more commendable than the decoration of the leopard's body.

### WHY MAY LOVED THE SQUIRRELS (57)

May loved all the things that God made. She told Him so, many, many times. She told Him how kind He is. He is kind because He puts so many good things all about us. May loved the squirrels. She liked to see them play. And they liked to come to her. They would take nuts from her hand. They would eat some. And they would put away others where no one could see them. One day May asked her mother why the squirrels put so many nuts away. Her mother said that they were doing what God wanted. May was glad to hear her mother say that. She had loved the squirrels before. She loved them even more now.

## Related Stories in "Teacher Tells a Story."

This story should be followed by stories 58 and 59. Other stories of similar thought matter are: 5, 60–65, inclusive, 135, 145, 146, 156–158, inclusive.

## Development of "Why May Loved the Squirrels."

*a.* Tell the children that it would not be advisable to invite a squirrel to a Hallowe'en party. He might not leave any nuts for the other guests to eat.

*b.* Say that the best nut-crackers that can be found are the teeth of the squirrel. Remark to yourself that it is difficult to have a squirrel around always when one needs a nut-cracker.

*c.* Remark that if the squirrels liked to come to you as they did to May, you might be able to coax one of them to live with you and be a nut-cracker for you.

*d.* Suddenly recall that the children are not familiar with the story of May and the squirrels. Say aloud that they would not like to hear it. Ask rhetorically if they would.   Upon assurance that they would, commence the story.

*e.* Bring out the fact that it was May's love of God and His creatures that made the animals so docile in coming to her.

*f.* Ask the children whether they love the squirrels more after learning of their obedience, than they did before.

## Dramatization.

*Two characters: May and her mother.*
*(Enter mother R.)*

MOTHER: May is a very good girl.   She loves the things that God has made.
*(Enter May L., skipping)*

MAY: O mother! Isn't God kind?

MOTHER: Yes, He is, my dear.

MAY: He puts so many good things here for us. And the squirrels.   How I love them, mother!

MOTHER: I am glad.   God made them, too.

MAY: They play with me.   They take nuts right out of my hand.

MOTHER: That shows they do not fear you.   They do not fear you because they know you love them.

MAY: But, mother, why do the squirrels put so many nuts away?   They never seem to have too many.

MOTHER: They are doing that because God wants them to.

MAY: O mother!   I love the squirrels more now than before.   They put the nuts away to do what God wants.

MOTHER: Yes, May.   But now my little girl must do something that God wants.   We must go to church this evening.   Come in, and let us get ready.
*(Exeunt both R.)*

**Silent Reading.** *Little Words in Big Words.*

Before the reading of the story in class, divide the class into two groups. The children are asked to find in one sentence at a time, as many little words in big words as possible. Show what you mean by a little word in a big word: "he" in "t-he." The child finding the greatest number in each sentence scores a point for his side. The purpose of this exercise is to help mental pronunciation, and the recognition of the elements of which a word is compounded. Without these qualities silent reading can not be more than a scanning of symbols. The words that should be found by the pupils in this story are indicated below, with the number of the sentence preceding. We have not considered "a" a word. The teacher may use her judgment, provided she be consistent.

1—love-d, t-he, t-h-at; 2—s-he, t-old, m-an-y, man-y; 3—s-he, t-old; 4—be-cause, m-an-y, ab-out; 5—love-d, t-he; 6—s-he, like-d, t-he-m, p-lay; 7—t-he-y, like-d, he-r; 8—t-he-y, fro-m, he-r, h-an-d; 9—t-he-y, e-at, so-me; 10—t-he-y, o-the-rs, a-way, w-h-ere, on-e, t-he-m; 11—on-e, as-k-ed, he-r, moth-er, t-he, m-an-y, a-way; 12—he-r, moth-er, s-aid, t-h-at, t-he-y, w-ere, do-in-g; 13—w-as, g-lad, h-ear, he-r, moth-er, t-h-at; 14—s-he, love-d, t-he, be-for-e; 15—s-he, love-d, t-he-m, eve-n.

**Related Stories from Other Sources.**

When God commanded Moses at the burning bush to go into the land of Egypt and to lead the Israelites out of bondage, Moses did not know how it was to be done, but he said that he would obey, and he did obey (Exodus, iii).

St. John Berchmans (August 13), a Jesuit, made a great deal of the very least things. He was faithful in little things. His obedience reached to details.

St. Robert of Molesmes (April 29) obtained permission from the Papal Legate in France to leave the monastery where he lived, in order to found a monastery with stricter rules. After living in this new monastery twelve years he was told to go back to his former home. This he did meekly, without a murmur.

Captain Lawrence, of the Chesapeake, was faithful to death in the naval battle with the Shannon, and in his dying moments cried, "Don't give up the ship."

"The Tree in the City" (in "Golden Windows," Richards) pictures the obedience of a tree in the midst of a city, growing and budding in obedience to God's will, unconcerned as to the reason for God's command. The story shows how in doing God's will, the tree brought consolation and joy to a sick child.

### THE LITTLE PUPPY (64)

There was once a little puppy. His name was Teddy. He liked to run after moving things. His mother told him one day that he might be hurt, if he did it again. He told himself to keep on doing it. One day he saw something new. It was coming towards him. A man was sitting on it. The seat was on top of two round things. These round things were moving along the ground. Teddy ran out to have some fun. He came too near one of the round things. It hit him, and he fell. He got up, and ran to his mother. He did as his mother told him after that.

## Related Stories in "Teacher Tells a Story."

This story should be followed by stories 65–68, inclusive.

## Development of "The Little Puppy."

a. Ask the children if they were ever in a street car or an automobile when a dog or a puppy ran out barking at the car or the machine; say that if they were, they must have thought the dog very foolish. Think aloud and say that automobiles can not be good to eat; then reconsider, and say that perhaps the dog is calling to the machine that he wants to run it a race, and that he will bet his last bone that he will win. Then, you might add that this can not interest an automobile because automobiles do not like bones, and would not know what to do with them. As another possibility you might suggest that the automobile may have run over the dog on a previous occasion, and that now he is trying to get revenge.

b. Say that you know of a little puppy who liked to run after cars and moving things, just for the fun of racing them. Say that he must have imagined himself to be very fast. Remark that he wanted, perhaps, to show his speed to everybody.

c. This will bring you to the story proper. In the mother dog's correction, have her call on her experience, and make her recite instances of what happened to other puppies who acted as Teddy was acting.

d. There is an opportunity to introduce humor in describing Teddy's conceit; say, for instance, that his chest swelled out like a paper bag full of air, ready to burst, when he thought of how much faster he was than the other dogs of whom his mother spoke.

e. Create suspense in describing the accident; make Teddy come close to the wheel several times before he is actually struck.

f. Emphasize the fact that it was to his mother he ran after the accident. Remark that the paper bag had burst. Say it was a good thing, as it resulted in Teddy's good resolution.

**Dramatization.**

*Two boys play the characters, John and William.*

JOHN: There is a fine horse and wagon!

WILLIAM: Look how fast it is coming!

JOHN: Where did that puppy come from?

WILLIAM: He just now ran out into the street.

JOHN: Look how close he is coming to the wheels.

WILLIAM: *(as both give a start)* I thought he was hit that time.

JOHN: So did I. *(They start again).* He will be hit, if he gets so close to those wheels.

WILLIAM: *(as they are startled a third time)* Well, he was hit that time. Did you see him fall?

JOHN: And do you hear him bark?

WILLIAM: There, the mother dog is licking him with her tongue.

JOHN: I think he will not run after moving wheels again.

WILLIAM: I hope he has made up his mind that way.
*(Exeunt both R.)*

**Silent Reading.** *The Queen's Visitors.*

Before the story is read in class the teacher assigns one sentence to each of fifteen children. She asks each one to read his sentence thoroughly as they are to go to visit the queen, and tell her the story. The class is asked to read the lesson at the same time.

After three minutes they come to the front of the room where the teacher plays the queen. She asks them who they are. They say they are a story (answering in unison). The queen wants to know the story. So she asks questions that should bring responses from the children to whom she has assigned the sentences. The questions should be asked in the same order as that in which the sentences are arranged. If any of the visitors does not recognize the question as fitting his sentence, the first child in the seats who raises his hand to answer and answers correctly, becomes a queen's visitor in place of him who failed. If none respond, teacher answers herself, and goes on with the questions. After the story is told, the queen thanks the visitors by having the class pray for them.

### Related Stories from Other Sources.

Cain persisted in indulging in thoughts of hatred until he finally committed murder, killing his brother (Genesis, iv, 1–12).

St. Ignatius (July 31) found occasion in an injury to leave the army, the cause of his wound, and to be what God asked him to be.

Henry II, of England, permitted himself to speak injuriously of St. Thomas of Canterbury. The result was his soldiers killed St. Thomas, and the blood of the martyr rested on the king. But the king repented of his deed, and did penance at the tomb of St. Thomas.

"Raggylug" (in "How to tell Stories to Children," Bryant) tells of a little rabbit who was almost strangled to death by a snake, and this through disobedience to its mother. The mother arrived just in time to save its life.

### THE MOUSE AND THE MATCH (65)

A mother mouse lived under a house. She told her little mice about little bits of wood with red tops. These bits would burn, if mice ate them. They might burn the mice, too. One day one of the mice left his home. He went up into the house. He saw many of these bits of wood there. But he would not eat them. He looked for other things. But he came back to the wood. He did not eat any of it. He went away again. He came back. The red tops looked very good. He took one of the bits. He ate it. Fire came from it. The mouse was burned very badly. He ate no more of these bits of wood.

## Related Stories in "Teacher Tells a Story."

This story should be preceded by story 64; and followed by stories 66–68, inclusive.

## Development of "The Mouse and the Match."

*a.* Ask the children if they know what lollypops are; draw their attention to the similarity of appearance between lollypops and matches. Say that mice seem to like matches as well as children like lollypops. Remark that as lollypops sometimes make children sick, so matches, being poisonous, usually make mice sick. Add emphatically that if children ate such poison they might die.

*b.* Call attention to the second danger in playing with matches. Personify a match, and make it say impatiently that it is a shame to be kept in prison in a match box, when there is so much light locked up in one's heart. Make the match long for the coming of a liberator, who will let the light and the fire out by scratching the match's head. Remark to yourself that the match is not to be trusted, that once the light and fire are permitted to come forth, no one knows whither it will spread; it may fire a little girl's dress, or a curtain in a room, or the carpet on which a spark may fall. Think aloud and say that if you were a child you would allow the match to stay in prison, so that you might not be blamed for the damage it might cause after its head was scratched.

*c.* Say that a mother mouse knew how dangerous matches are; she knew that they are poisonous, but most of all that they can burn and destroy. This leads

directly to the story.   Be sure to emphasize the struggle
going on in the mouse's head between obedience and
the satisfaction of his appetite.   Note the gradual
yielding, brought about by frequent returns to the
matches.   Think aloud, and say that the only way
to overcome temptation is to stay away from it.   Cen-
sure the mouse for returning to the temptation.   Picture forcibly the mouse's awakening when the match
commences to burn; note his consternation.   Describe
his wild running about while his fur is afire.   Picture
his appearance after he succeeds in putting the fire
out by plunging into a pan of water (or in some other
fashion).   Do not forget to commend his resolution,
but add that if he is to eat no more matches, he must
remain away from them.

## Dramatization.

*A boy and a girl play the characters.*

BOY: Did you put all the matches back in the box?

GIRL: All that I could find.

BOY: Well, I hope you found them all.

GIRL: Why?

BOY: Because mice may get at them, if you did not.

GIRL: What can mice do with them?

BOY: They can try to eat them.   That will make fire
come from them.

GIRL *(screams):* There is a mouse now!

BOY: He will not hurt you.   But I hope he does not
find any matches.

GIRL: Look there *(points)!*   There is something on
fire, now.

BOY *(runs L. and steps on imaginary match):* Yes,
and here are more matches.   You did not pick them all
up.   *(Stoops and picks up the imaginary matches.)*

GIRL: Did that mouse make it burn?

BOY: He must have. I hope he was burned himself. Then he would not eat matches again. But come, I think there are some matches in the next room. We must pick them up, too.

*(Exeunt both L.)*

**Silent Reading.** *Mixed Sentences.*

After the story has been read in class, divide the class into two groups. Have children combine words as directed by teacher, who gives them the number of the word according to its order in the story. The first to have the meaning of the combination scores a point for his group. The purpose of this exercise is to show that the words in the story are dynamic, and not confined to the function they enjoy in any given sentence.

Examples of combinations, the figures being the numbers of the words according to the order of their occurrence in this story:

*1, 2, 3, 41, 43* means "A mother mouse left home."

*8, 9, 28, 29, 31* means "She told them they burn."

*37, 38, 39, 40, 72, 73* means "One of the mice came back."

**Related Stories from Other Sources.**

Daniel and his companions refused to eat the forbidden food which Nabuchodonosor had assigned them. After ten days they appeared more comely on a humble diet than they who ate of the king's table (Daniel I). The reward of self-restraint is shown in this narrative.

St. Thomas Aquinas (March 7) is an example of stability, and of resistance to repeated temptation, since he overcame the almost insuperable opposition of his family to his becoming a religious.

"Horatius at the Bridge" ("Fifty Famous Stories Retold," Baldwin), inculcates constancy in showing how

Horatius kept the Etruscans at bay, while the guards behind him hewed down the bridge that would have given the enemy entrance to their town.

### DOROTHY'S ROSES (72)

Many years ago, boys and girls were killed for loving God. They could not hear Mass in houses made for God. They had to make big holes down under the ground. There they would hear Mass, where no one could see them. Dorothy lived at that time. She loved God. She went to Mass. The soldiers asked her not to go to Mass any more. She said she would always go. It was right for Dorothy to go to Mass. The soldiers were bad for telling her not to go. They said they would kill her. She said she would go to Heaven, then. She said she would send them roses, when she should get to Heaven. After they killed Dorothy, a little boy came with roses for them. They were from Dorothy.

### Related Stories in "Teacher Tells a Story."

This story should be preceded by stories 60–71, inclusive; and followed by stories 73 and 74.

### Development of "Dorothy's Roses."

*a.* Ask the children what they would do if some Sunday morning as they were about to enter the church, a soldier would stop them and point his gun at them telling them that they must not go into church. Think aloud and say that you believe they would run home as fast as their heels could carry them, to have their parents come to church with them for protection.

*b.* Say that long ago, bad people would not allow Catholics to have churches; that when the latter dug holes down under the ground, the bad people sent soldiers to find out where these holes were. Tell them that the Catholics at that time never knew when they would be met at the opening of the hole in the ground by a soldier sent to arrest them.

*c.* Note the courage of the people, who in spite of the danger would not stay home from Mass.

*d.* The story proper may be commenced here. You may show how Dorothy was arrested one day as she was about to assist at Mass. Say that the soldiers tried to make her promise that she would not go to Mass again. Show that she could not make a promise of that kind without implicitly denying her faith. Show that the soldiers are impressed by her courage; that they believe her faith must have some power in it of which they are ignorant. Make them falter in their resolve to kill one so beautiful and young; but show that evil wins the struggle, and that Dorothy is put to death.

*e.* Create a scene in which one of the most irreverent of the soldiers is joking about Dorothy's promise; have him say, for instance, that she must have been talking in her sleep, imagining that she was going to a garden of flowers; have the other soldiers interested in what he is saying; interrupt him by having the little boy tap him on the back; have all the other soldiers gasp with astonishment, and show him crestfallen. End by having one of the more serious soldiers reflect that he is disgusted with the persecution of the innocent Catholics, and that he does not want to have any more to do with it; have him take one of the roses and say that he will keep it always to remind him of Dorothy's courage, and to make him courageous, too.

## Dramatization.

*Five large boys play the soldiers, a girl plays Dorothy, and a sixth boy, of low stature, plays the little boy.*

*Scene I. Five soldiers in group.*

FIRST SOLDIER: We will catch many of them today.

SECOND SOLDIER: Yes, they do not know we have found their hole.

THIRD SOLDIER: It will be great fun for us.

FOURTH SOLDIER: We will make them pray.

FIFTH SOLDIER: You may think it's fun, but I do not.

THIRD SOLDIER: Are you one of them, too?

FIFTH SOLDIER: No, but I wish I were as brave as they are.

FOURTH SOLDIER: Ha! a soldier wishes he were brave as one of these rats.

FIRST SOLDIER: *(looking R.)* Here comes one of them, now.

SECOND SOLDIER: She is but a child.

FIRST SOLDIER: We should not kill a child.

SECOND SOLDIER: But we must make her say she will stop going to Mass.

FOURTH SOLDIER: And if she will not, we must kill her.

FIFTH SOLDIER: You can be a bear, if you want. I will not kill a child.

*(Enter Dorothy R.)*

FIRST SOLDIER: Where are you going, my little girl?

DOROTHY *(a little frightened)*: Why, I am going to—

SECOND SOLDIER: To Mass? Do not say no.

DOROTHY *(becoming braver)*: Yes, I was going to Mass.

FOURTH SOLDIER: I guess you pray like a parrot, too. Let us make her pray.

FIFTH SOLDIER: You will not while I am here.

DOROTHY: Kind soldier, I am praying for you and for him, even now.

FIRST SOLDIER: You know that we could kill you, don't you?

DOROTHY: I do not fear you.

SECOND SOLDIER: You need not fear us. We will let you go, but you must promise not to go to Mass again.

DOROTHY: I can not promise that. I must always go to Mass.

THIRD SOLDIER: We must kill you, then.

DOROTHY: If you do, you will send me to Heaven.

FOURTH SOLDIER: To Heaven! Ha! Ha! And what will you give us for sending you there?

DOROTHY: I have nothing to give you now but prayer; but when I get to Heaven I will send you roses.

FIRST SOLDIER: So you will not say that you will stop going to Mass?

DOROTHY: I can not.

FIRST SOLDIER: Then come with us. But think again; we do not want to kill a brave girl like you.

DOROTHY: I must always go to Mass.

FIRST SOLDIER: Come on, then.

*(Exeunt all L.)*

*Scene II. Five soldiers in group.*

FIFTH SOLDIER: Well, you saw that she was brave till the end, didn't you?

FIRST SOLDIER: Yes, I could hardly make myself strike her.

FOURTH SOLDIER: Ha! She was only dreaming. *(Enter little boy R., who walks slowly towards group, carrying basket.)* She was talking in her sleep; she was dreaming that she was walking into a flower garden.

*(Little boy taps Fourth Soldier on the back; this soldier turns around chagrined; little boy offers basket; all soldiers show surprise).*

LITTLE BOY: Dorothy sends them to you.

*(Little boy exits R.)*

FIRST SOLDIER: She must be in Heaven.

FIFTH SOLDIER: I knew she would keep her word. But where is the little boy? Come, we must follow him, and learn more of her.

*(Exeunt all R.)*

**Silent Reading.** *Guessing Pantomimes.*

Before the story is read in class, various scenes in the story are acted by specially drilled groups of children, whereupon the children search through the story to find what scene has been acted. The class prays to Saint Dorothy for the one who first discovers the sentence which describes the pantomime. The purpose of this exercise is to impress on the child's mind the relation between action and the description of it.

Suggested pantomimes:

Six boys digging, showing action of both pick and shovel (digging the catacombs).

Twelve boys and girls kneeling devoutly with hands clasped (hearing Mass).

Boy offering imaginary basket to five other boys (the offering of Dorothy's roses).

**Related Stories from Other Sources.**

The companions of Daniel undergo the punishment of the fiery furnace rather than worship the idols of Nabuchodonosor (Daniel, iii, 12–24).

St. Gregory VII (May 25) upon his election to the See of St. Peter called upon all the pastors of the Catholic world to lay down their lives rather than betray the laws of God to the will of princes. He himself practised what he preached, was wounded and cast into prison by the Cenci in Rome, and died in exile into which he was driven by the Emperor of Germany, Henry IV, after the latter had set up an anti-pope.

St. Peter Martyr (April 29), a Dominican, asked our Lord at Mass that he might die for Him. He was granted his request. The heretics against whom he preached lay in wait for him, and struck his head with an ax. Before he died Peter dipped his finger in his own blood and wrote on the sand, "I believe in God, Creator of heaven and earth."

"Casabianca" ("Fifty Famous Stories Retold," Baldwin), the son of the captain of a doomed vessel, remained in the position in which his father had placed him, awaiting his father's word to leave. His father had been killed in the battle; and his son died when the ship was blown to bits.

The American forces at Valley Forge during the Revolutionary War give an example of constancy to a cause that can not be without its effect in stimulating constancy to faith.

"The Oxen and the Axle-Trees" (Aesop's Fables) contrasts the constant suffering of the burdened oxen with the whining of the axles, that are not laboring nearly so hard as the beasts.

### PROUD JEAN (76)

Jean is a good girl. She works very hard in school. She can read very well. One day Sister said she wanted all the boys and girls to do their best. A man was coming to see what they could do. When the man came, he asked the boys and girls to tell him things. Most of the boys and girls did well. But Jean did not know anything. She went home crying. That night as she was sleeping, God told her something. He told her why she did not know anything that day. It was because she was proud. She worked hard, but she did not ask Him to help her. No one can do well if God does not help him.

### Related Stories in "Teacher Tells a Story."

This story should be followed by stories 77–79, inclusive. Other stories of similar thought matter are: 80–82, inclusive.

### Development of "Proud Jean."

*a.* Refer to some good reading that has been done by the class, and say that you are sure the children must have asked God to help them before that lesson began. Remark that unless God had been helping them they would have been unable to do so well.

*b.* Say that you know the story of a little girl who forgot to ask God to help her. Ask if the children would like to hear it. When they answer in the affirmative, tell the story of "Proud Jean."

*c.* In telling about the examination by the visitor bring in examples from reading and spelling, and from arithmetic, if the children have commenced to work in it. Make the answers of Jean as ludicrous as possible. This will introduce interesting humor, and at the same time show how foolish we can be without God's help.

*d.* When she arrives home, have her mother sympathize with her; but let the mother ask if she prayed to God for help, thus laying the foundation for the dream.

*e.* The dream should be a reproduction of Christ's rebuking the disciples for driving the children away from the audience that was listening to Him. Make Jean one of the group. Do not betray to the children who the Teacher is, until He speaks to Jean, and tells her the reason for her failure. This will sustain interest in the children, who will be anxious to discover His identity, even if they do suspect it.

*f.* Think aloud and say that dreams should not be necessary to make children know that they depend on God for everything. Their knowledge that He made them should be sufficient.

## Dramatization.

*A large girl takes the part of Jean's mother; and a small one, the part of Jean.*

*Scene I. (Enter Jean and her mother R., Jean crying).*

JEAN: Mother, I did not know a thing.

MOTHER: After all the work you did last night!

JEAN: When the man asked me about things, I could not say any of them.

MOTHER: What did the man say?

JEAN: He did not say anything. But he must think I do not know much.

MOTHER: Jean, I think I know why you could not do the things you wanted to do.

JEAN: Do you, Mother? Why?

MOTHER: Did you ask God to help you last night?

JEAN: I prayed before I went to bed.

MOTHER: But did you ask God to be with you when the man would ask you about things?

JEAN: No, Mother, I did not.

MOTHER: I think that is why you could not tell the man the things he wanted to know. But, come, you must go to your room, and tell God that you will not forget again to ask His help.

(Exeunt both L.)

*Scene II. Next morning. (Enter Jean and her mother L.)*

MOTHER: Well, dear, how are you this morning?

JEAN: I feel much better, Mother. Our Lord spoke to me last night.

MOTHER: Our Lord spoke to you! You were dreaming.

JEAN: Yes, Our Lord spoke to me in a dream.

MOTHER: What did He say to you?

JEAN: He told me many things. He told me that He loves me. And you were right, Mother.

MOTHER: What do you mean, Jean?

JEAN: You said that I could not tell the man what he wanted to know because I did not ask God to help me.

MOTHER: Yes, I did say that.

JEAN: Well, Our Lord told me that is so. He wants me to ask Him for help in everything I do.

MOTHER: We will not forget that this morning at Mass, will we, Jean. We must be going, or we shall be late. Come, Jean. And don't forget to ask God's help this morning.

JEAN: I shall never forget that again, Mother.

*(Exeunt both R.)*

## Silent Reading. *Playing Teacher.*

Before reading the lesson in class, divide the class into two groups. Take sentence by sentence, and have the children read them silently. They are told in advance that after they have read each sentence they may ask teacher a question which will require as an answer the sentence they have read. They raise their hands as they have the questions ready. The first to ask a really pertinent question for each sentence scores a point for this group. The purpose of this exercise is to familiarize the children with changing the same thought from the declarative to the interrogative form.

### Related Stories from Other Sources.

God confounded the workers on the Tower of Babel, because of their proud trust in themselves (Genesis, xi, 1–9).

The studies of St. Peter Damian (February 23) were sanctified by vigils, fasts, and prayers. In spite of his learning, he remained an example of humility all his life.

Dionysius the Great (November 17), Bishop of Alexandria, though one of the most learned of the Fathers, distrusted his will power in the matter of reading heretical works. He was reassured by a vision in which Our Lord told him that he might read all that came to his hand, as he would be strong enough, with God's grace, to be true to the Faith.

Luther's desire to parade his learning led him to revolt against the authority of the Pope.

"The Lamp" (Aesop's Fables) tells how a gust of wind put out a lamp that boasted it gave more light than the sun.

"The Gnat and the Bull" (Aesop's Fables) describes the lighting of a gnat upon the horn of a bull, his remaining there for a time, and finally his buzzing to attract the bull's attention. The bull remarks laconically that he did not even know that the gnat had come, and that he would not miss the gnat when he would go.

"To-morrow" (in "Golden Windows," Richards) represents two spirits in the Land of To-morrow; one fearful, the other brave. The fearful spirit was proud in the land of to-day; the brave spirit, humble.

### SAVED BY A MOTHER (74)

John was seen taking a pear that was not his. James saw him. James did not want him to take it. James made John come back to his house. He wanted to send John to jail. Just then James' mother came in. John said he would not take anything that way again. The mother asked James to let John go. James did what his mother asked. We hurt Jesus when we do bad things, as John hurt James. The mother of Jesus will be like James' mother. She will ask Jesus to let us go, if we want to keep away from sin. And Jesus will do it, because He loves His mother.

## Related Stories in "Teacher Tells a Story."

This story should be followed by stories 83, and 86–89, inclusive. Other stories of similar thought matter are: 80–82, inclusive.

## Development of "Saved by a Mother."

*a.* Remind the children that when they have had a good day in school or have made a good mark, they think first of mother. The reason for this, you will tell them, is that they wish mother to take part in their happiness; they love their mothers, and wish to make them happy.

*b.* Tell the children that this love of mother makes people do many good things, when they are asked to do them by their mothers. Say that you heard one time about a man who forgave a thief because his mother begged him to do so.

*c.* Make a great deal out of the chase to catch the thief. You can make this exciting, and it will serve to arouse those who may be inattentive. You may introduce many details; have one or other fall; have them narrowly escape being hit by an automobile; bring a policeman on the scene. A little humor may be introduced by describing the countenances of the bystanders; or make some of them join the chase and do ludicrous things.

*d.* Have John plead long with the mother before she intercedes for him; make James unwilling at first to listen to his mother. Both these pleas give an opportunity for creating suspense in the children's minds as to how the story will end.

*e.* Think aloud and say that you would have done what James did, if your mother had asked you. Remark that you would not make stealing right by doing that; but that you would forgive the thief because he was sorry.

*f.* Emphasize the great love of Christ for His Blessed Mother. Reflect that you will always have great confidence in her, because Christ does what she asks Him. Ask the children how many of them will ask Mary to help them in their troubles.

### Dramatization.

*Two boys play James and John; a girl plays the mother.*

JOHN: So you will not let me go.

JAMES: No, the policeman is waiting outside and you must go with him.

*(Enter James' mother R.)*

MOTHER: Why, James, what is going on?

JAMES: This man stole some of my bread, mother.

JOHN: But I had not eaten for a long time. Won't you please let me go? *(Turning to James' mother).* Won't you help me? He is your boy. Ask him to let me go.

MOTHER: Why didn't you ask him for some bread?

JOHN: I asked so many people who said no, that I thought he would say no, also.

MOTHER: But you should have asked to see what he would say. If you are set free this time, you will steal again.

JOHN: Never.  I will die first.

MOTHER: James, did you hear what he says.  He will not steal again.  I think you should let him go.

JAMES: Yes, and have him come back to-night, and steal all I have.

MOTHER: Look at his face.  I know he means what he says.

JAMES: They all say they will not steal again, to get free.

MOTHER: But this man means it.  If you cannot see that he does, believe your mother.

JAMES: All right, mother, he can go.  It is because you ask.

JOHN: Thank you, sir, thank you!  I will keep my word!  And I thank you, too *(turning to James' mother)* for what you have done for me.

**Silent Reading.** *Finding the Magic Sentence.*

Before the story is read in class, write one of the sentences on a slip of paper, and hide it very ceremoniously in a book.  Ask the children then to read the story silently, and to tell you which of the sentences they think you have hidden away.  Offer a holy picture for the winner.  To be eligible for the prize, the children must give the reason for their selection, or at least give the meaning of the sentence they choose.

**Related Stories from Other Sources.**

King Antiochus knew the power of mother love when he asked the Mother of the Macchabees to persuade her last living son to disobey the law of God.  She on the contrary confirmed him in his resolution to obey, and she won victory in his martyrdom (II Macchabees, vii, 25–29).

The influence of mothers over their sons is to be

seen also in the case of St. Monica (May 4), whose early instructions together with her prayers resulted in the conversion of her son, St. Augustine.

St. Elizabeth of Portugal (July 8) acted effectively on several occasions between her husband and her son, Alphonso, who had taken up arms against his father.

The mother of Prince Gallitzin, through her influence with her son, persuaded him to be a fervent Catholic when he was about seventeen. She participated therefore in the great work that her son did later in America, because it was she who caused him to be devout at the beginning of his career.

"The Apron String" (in "Golden Windows," Richards) shows how useful it is even for grown men to have at least a little of their mothers' apron strings about them to save them in the face of disaster.

" 'Go' and 'Come' " (in "Golden Windows," Richards) contrasts driving with leading, but makes the mother the master in the matter of persuasion.

## MY ROBIN FRIENDS (91)

I love the robin. I love the robin because God made him. I love the mother robin. I love the father robin. I love the little robins. I love them all. They all come from God. But God made the robins just to live here. He wants them to sing and fly. He wants them to make little boys and girls happy. That is all He made them for. But God made me for something more than that. He wants me to sing. He wants me to make boys and girls happy. He wants me to love my father and my mother. But He wants to give me something better than all that. He wants me to live with Him forever.

## Related Stories in "Teacher Tells a Story."

This story should be preceded by story 90; and followed by stories 92–96, inclusive.

**Development of "My Robin Friends."**

*a.* Make an interest contact by telling of an occasion when you were entertained by a robin. You may introduce some humor here by saying that the robin paused in his song to see whether you would applaud, or at least whether you were paying strict attention. You may note that he hopped about from limb to limb of a bush to get a better view of your face in order to see whether his singing was appreciated. Note, if you wish, that you commenced to sing quietly, and that the robin chirped louder than ever, in order that you would have to hear him over your own voice.

*b.* Say, that the robin delights to amuse boys and girls. Say it is one of the things for which God made him. Reflect and say that you love the robin for his song, but most of all because it was God who made him and sent him to cheer boys and girls.

*c.* Ask the children if they have ever been entertained by a robin. Have one of them describe his reaction to the robin's song, if possible. Ask them if they ever saw a choir of robins. Ask yourself if a choir of robins ought to have a teacher or a director. Answer your own question by saying that God is their director, and that they need no other teacher.

*d.* Remark the obedience of the robin, and wonder whether boys and girls do as God wants, as the robin does. Then, say by way of afterthought, "But what does God want boys and girls to do?" The avenue is now open to you to describe as many duties as you wish, always driving home the necessity of obedience by referring to the robin's song.

**Dramatization.**

*A little boy and a little girl play the characters. (Enter both children R.)*

BOY: Do you hear the robin sing?

GIRL: Yes, and there is the robin over there in the bush.

BOY: Do you see how he looks at us?

GIRL: Yes, he wants to know how we like his song.

BOY: We like it very much, Mr. Robin.

GIRL: Yes, we do.

BOY: I think he understands us.

GIRL: Yes, because he is singing louder than before.

BOY: He is doing that to please us.

GIRL: All robins sing to make boys and girls happy.

BOY: Who teaches them to sing?

GIRL: You know as well as I do. Why, God teaches them to sing.

BOY: He teaches them to sing, just to make us happy, doesn't He?

GIRL: Yes. And they do what He tells them. They sing for us.

BOY: I love the robin for being so good and kind.

GIRL: And so do I. I am going to be like the robin.

BOY: And so am I.

GIRL: Come, let us sit on that bench near the bush, where we can see and hear him better.

*(Exeunt both L.)*

**Silent Reading.** *Climbing the Ladder.*

Before the story is read in class, divide the class into two groups. Tell children to read the story silently, and to raise their hands as they finish. Note the order in which the children raise their hands. When all have finished, ask them in the order they finished to tell the meaning of the sentences, beginning from the end, or from the last sentence. Count seventeen for the child who gives the meaning of the last sentence, sixteen for him who tells the sense of the next to the last, and so on.

### Related Stories from Other Sources.

God's love for creation, and especially for human souls, is shown in the story of Jonas and the Ivy (Jonas, iv).

St. Francis of Assisi (October 4) used to call the dumb animals his brothers and sisters.

St. Peter Nolasco (January 31) realized the value to God of human souls, toiling for twenty-five years for the Spanish slaves under the yoke of the Moors, in many cases converting even their Mohammedan masters.

Father Jacques Marquette, S. J., showed a like appreciation in his labors among the Indians of the Mississippi valley; as did Father Bartholomew Las Casas for the overburdened Indians of the Antilles.

"The Kingdoms" ("Fifty Famous Stories Retold," Baldwin) tells of Frederick William, King of Prussia, and his questioning a little girl about the kingdom to which he belonged (expecting the answer, "to the animal kingdom"). The reply was, "to the Kingdom of Heaven."

### THE SONG OF THE ROBIN (98)

The robin sings three times. Then it looks around. It is looking for something to eat. It wants to take something good to the little robins. Why does the robin sing three times? What does the robin do when it sings? It says things to God that He likes to hear. To what Persons do we say things, when we tell anything to God? We say them to God the Father. We say them to God the Son. We say them to God the Holy Ghost. They are the same Persons I talk about when I bless myself. Now, why does the robin sing three times? Because it is talking to the three Persons in God.

**Related Stories in "Teacher Tells a Story."**

This story should be preceded by story 97, and followed by stories 99 and 100.

**Development of "The Song of the Robin."**

*a.* Tell of a dish of strawberry ice cream; describe how delicious it looks; then say that it was given to a little girl friend of yours by her mother. Ask the children if they think the child in question placed the dish of cream on the table, and went to the piano to play a selection before eating it. Ask them if they think she sang a little song, leaving the ice cream to wait until she finished singing.

*b.* You may answer for them, and say that she did neither of these things. You may hint that she did something else before eating, and that you will tell them what it was before the story is finished. This will secure attention to the end.

*c.* Say now that you saw a robin one day singing, while a nice big worm lay right in front of him. And add that worms to robins are as delicious as ice cream is to children. Ask yourself why a robin would sing before eating, while children will not?

*d.* Ask yourself again why the robin sings *three* times before he eats. Answer your question, and say that the robin is praying, that he is saying his prayer before meals. Go on, and say that the robin sings three times in the morning when he commences the day. Repeat the question, "Why does he sing *three* times?" and give the explanation as it stands in the story. Before concluding say that your little friend asked God to bless the ice cream before she ate it; you promised to give this explanation in the beginning.

**Dramatization.**

*A boy and a girl play the characters.*
*(Enter boy and girl L.)*
GIRL: Look at that robin hopping about on the ground.
BOY: Yes, he has just found a worm.
GIRL: Is he going to eat it?
BOY: I do not know. I think so.
GIRL: He is singing. He must not want to eat it.
BOY: Hear him! He is singing three times.
GIRL: Now he is eating the worm.
BOY: I wonder why he sang three times.
GIRL: He was praying before eating.
BOY: But why did he sing *three* times?
GIRL: Because he did not want to sing two.
BOY: No, because he wanted to pray to God the Father, to God the Son, and to God the Holy Ghost.
GIRL: I did not know that robins pray to God.
BOY: They do what God tells them.
GIRL: I will always pray before eating, too.
BOY: And to God the Father, to God the Son, and to God the Holy Ghost. Come, now, it is nearly supper time. We will soon pray to these Three Persons. I hope you do not forget how the robin prays.
*(Exeunt both R.)*

**Silent Reading.** *Leap Frog.*

Before the story is read in class, divide the class into two groups. Tell them that they are going to play leap frog, jumping over every other word, jumping over the first word in each sentence. Have the children read sentence by sentence. As soon as they discover all the words they are to jump over in a given sentence, they are to raise their hands. The child who first names all the words that he jumped scores a point for his side.

## Related Stories from Other Sources.

Abraham visited by three men in the vale of Mambre, addresses the three: "Lord if I have found favor in thy sight, pass not away from thy servant," recognizing the Three Persons as One Lord (Genesis, xviii, 1–5).

St. Hilary of Poitiers, a convert from paganism, opposed the enemies of the Trinity in the French Councils, and was banished to Phrygia on account of false accusations made to the emperor by his enemies. In exile he wrote his great work on the Trinity (January 14).

St. Augustine (August 28), a defender of the Trinity, is said to have been puzzling over this Mystery on the seashore one day, when he saw a boy digging in the sand. As he watched, the lad later carried bucket after bucket of water and poured it into the hole he had dug. St. Augustine asked what he was trying to do. The lad said he was going to empty the ocean into the hole. The Saint remarked that it would be impossible. Whereupon the child said that it would be no more impossible to do that than to get an understanding of the Trinity into the head of Augustine.

### THE ROSE BUSH (113)

Once upon a time a seed was put under the ground. It could not see anything there. But it grew just the same. One day a little green head could be seen above the ground. It was a little rose bush looking for light. The seed was now the rose bush. It would not stay under the ground. It came above the ground to make boys and girls happy. After Our Lord died on the cross, they put Him under the ground. But He had told His boys and girls that He would not stay there. So He came back to them after three days and three nights. He came to make them happy.

### Related Stories in "Teacher Tells a Story."

This story should be preceded by story 112; and followed by stories 114-118 inclusive, and 120-123 inclusive.

### Development of "The Rose Bush."

*a.* Create interest by asking the children whether they have ever examined dried peas or beans. Remark that inside, tucked between the two halves, they will find a little fish tail. This fish tail is really two small leaves ready to grow as soon as the pea or bean is placed in the ground. They will not stay there, buried deep, but will commence to grow, pushing themselves up through the dirt until they arrive at the top. Then they push right through, to see the light. They will then grow into bean or pea stalks.

*b.* Say that you heard of a seed that belonged to a much more beautiful family than the peas or the beans. When it was placed under the ground it would not stay either. Tell the story as it is found in the book. You may speak of the soliloquies of the seed while it is under ground, when it first pushes its head above ground, when it sees the children. Hope should be the keynote of these reflections; as well as love for God, and for boys and girls. Ask the children when you have finished if they do not think the rose is more beautiful than peas or beans. Remark, however, that all are pleasing to God when they do the work He asks of them.

*c.* Make the comparison between the changed state of the seed when it appears above ground, with the

changed state of Our Lord's body. Show that He
arose of His own power, while the seed rises through
God's assistance. Show that Our Lord came back to
cheer up His friends, and to make them willing to do
great things for Him.

## Dramatization.

*A boy and a girl take the characters. (Enter boy and
girl R.)*

BOY: I want to see if my little seed is growing.

GIRL: When did you put it in the ground?

BOY: Many days ago, I put it there. I have been
coming every day to see if it has put its head above
the ground.

GIRL: What makes the seed grow?

BOY: Don't you know? Why God makes it grow.
He gives it things to eat.

GIRL: Why does God want it to grow?

BOY: He wants it to make us happy.

*(They both walk towards L.)*

BOY: If it has not put its head above the ground, I
think I will dig down to see if it is growing.

GIRL: No, you must wait.

BOY: *(shouts and waves arms with glee)* No, I must
not wait. There it is, it has come up to see the light.
See how strong it looks!

*(Both bend over to look at bush).*

GIRL: I am sure we shall be more happy when it grows
higher.

BOY: We shall, all right. But, come, we must make
mother happy, now; we must tell her that the seed has
grown, and pushed its head above the ground.

*(Exeunt both R.)*

**Silent Reading.** *Musical Words.*

After reading the story in class, divide the class into two groups. Say to the class that certain words sounded musical to you when they were read. Say that you are going to tell them to the class one at a time. That they must try to find how often that musical sound occurred in the story. The child first finding the correct number of times, scores a point for his side. This drill will familiarize the child with the printed form of the words, and will give him practice in enlarging his eye sweep of the printed page.

Words suggested in this story, with the number of times they occur:

The—8, it—5, ground—5, he—4, came—3, not—3, under—3, three—2, happy—2, boys—2, girls—2, them—2, little—2.

**Related Stories from Other Sources.**

Ezechiel had a vision of the resurrection of dry bones, foreshadowing the deliverance of the people of Israel from captivity, as well as the resurrection of the body (Ezechiel, xxxvii, 1-14).

"Bruce and the Spider" ("Fifty Famous Stories Retold," Baldwin) shows the resurrection of hope in Bruce after seeing the perseverance of the spider in weaving her web.

"The Little Pink Rose" ("Stories to Tell Children," Bryant) personifies the Sun and the Wind, both of which assist the pink rose in coming up to the light from its burial place beneath the ground.

"Why the Morning Glory Climbs" ("How to Tell Stories to Children," Bryant) explains that the morning glory came to climb because it wanted to show its face to a little injured wren away up in a tree. This story is sufficiently connected with resurrection to be apropos.

"Baby Seed Song" ("The Posy Ring," Wiggin-Smith) is song of a seed to its brother under the ground.

## MOTHER'S HELPER (125)

Mother robin is kind to the little robins. But your mother is much more kind to you. Mother likes her boys and girls to eat things hot. She has to be near the fire a long time to make them hot. Hedwig's mother gave her a set of pots and pans. Hedwig loved her mother for that. Hedwig wanted to help her mother. Her mother told her to get her pots, and help. Hedwig found how hard it is to get things hot to eat. She was more kind to her mother after she found that out. She loved God more, too. She knew that He had given her this kind mother.

### Related Stories in "Teacher Tells a Story."

This story should be preceded by story 124; and followed by stories 126-128, inclusive.

### Development of "Mother's Helper."

*a.* Say that some children like to make noise; that they like to have horns and drums so that they can be hammering at the latter and blowing the former. Such children make drums, if they have not the real instrument, out of pans and pots, and anything that will make noise when it is struck. Introduce humor by exaggerating the noise.

*b.* Contrast this annoying tendency with that of the little girl in the story who knew how to use her toys to help, instead of to trouble, her mother.

*c.* Show the real discomfort in standing near a stove to cook; picture a woman in that position; describe her flushed cheeks, the labored breathing. Note that Hedwig had seen her mother cook many times, but had not observed the discomfort she endured in doing it.

*d.* There is an opportunity for humor in describing Hedwig's vain attempts to do things correctly. You can make her drop a pan on the cat's tail; have the milk bottle nearly upset, and show that when Hedwig caught it, some of it splashed out in her face; make her put two helpings of pepper in the potatoes instead of one each of salt and pepper. Maintain a humorous tone throughout, so that the children will not take these things too seriously. Reflect in the end that practice is required before one can do things well. Insist upon the lesson, missed by Hedwig previously, but now learned through difficult experience. Ask the children what they think of their mother's work for them.

**Dramatization.**

*Two girls play the characters: one, the mother; the other, Hedwig.*

Scene I. *(Enter Hedwig and her mother R.)*

HEDWIG: Mother, I thank you very much for the pots and pans.

MOTHER: I am glad you like them, dear.

HEDWIG: But I have not had much fun with them.

MOTHER: Why, how is that, dear?

HEDWIG: Well, you know I love you, don't you?

MOTHER: I know that, yes indeed. I know you do everything I ask. That shows you love me.

HEDWIG: But you never ask me to do what I would like to do.

MOTHER: What is that?

HEDWIG: I would like to help you to cook.

MOTHER: Very well, come with me; you may help me to-day.

*(Exeunt both R.)*

Scene II. *(Enter Hedwig and her mother R.; time is one hour later.)*

HEDWIG: My but I am glad it is all over.

MOTHER: Were you warm?

HEDWIG: I thought I was being cooked.

MOTHER: That is because you have not cooked before.

HEDWIG: I know now how hard you have to work for me, mother. I love you more than I ever did.

MOTHER: And I love my little Hedwig more, too. *(Looks off L.)* But here comes your daddy, we must go to meet him.

*(Exeunt both L.)*

**Silent Reading.** *Street Car Signs.*

Before the story is read in class, divide the class into two groups. Tell the children they are riding in a street car. The sentences in the story are signs in the street car. Ask the children to read the first sign, and so on, sentence by sentence. The child who first explains the sign correctly scores a point for his group.

**Related Stories from Other Sources.**

The mother of Moses used all her prudence in caring for her son in order that he might not be put to death according to Pharaoh's order (Exodus, ii, 1-10).

St. Bridget of Sweden (October 8) devoted herself to the care of her eight children, particularly to their spiritual training. One of them, Catherine, became a saint.

St. Hedwig (October 17) also was a devoted mother. Her son, Duke Henry, was surnamed the Pious because of his life which she was instrumental in guiding. Her daughter, Gertrude, became abbess of the Cistercian convent at Trebnitz.

The common people of Rome erected a monument in

Rome to Cornelia, the mother of the Gracchi, the champions of the people, for the part she had in training them.

"About Angels" (in "Golden Windows," Richards) shows how a mother is an angel who cares for her child when no one else will be troubled with it.

### BREAD FROM HEAVEN (129)

Long ago God's friends were going from one home to another. This was before God the Son came from His home to die for us. God's friends had nothing to eat. There was nothing growing for them. They thought they were going to die. But God saw they had nothing to eat. He did not want them to die. He wanted them to live, and go to their new home. So every day He sent down from His home very good bread. It came down like rain. The boys and girls went out to eat it. Their mothers said they could not make such good bread. No one can make bread so well as God can.

### Related Stories in "Teacher Tells a Story."

This story should be followed by stories 130-137, inclusive.

### Development of "Bread from Heaven."

*a.* Ask the children if they have ever seen sparrows fly about in search of crumbs in the winter time. Say to them that if they want to bring these birds to their window sills when the snow is on the ground all they need do is spread some bread crumbs there. The sparrows find it difficult to get food during the winter. It is hard to find worms and seeds, and as a result they would starve if they could not pick up bits of food discarded by human beings.

*b.* Say that a long time ago God's friends were without food in their travels. Tell the children it was not the cold, but the heat, that prevented things from growing in the desert through which they were passing.

*c.* Continue the story, laying special emphasis on the coming of the manna. Develop a dramatic situation by making the people cry that they can not live another day without food; show that many are fainting from hunger. In the midst of this misery, describe the falling of the manna. Make the Israelites mistake it for hail. Have the murmur that it is not bad enough to be starving, they must be afflicted in addition by a storm. Let one of the curious children of the Israelites pick up a piece of the manna, look at it, put it in his mouth, and then shout with joy that it is good to eat. Picture the happiness in the camp of the Israelites when the adults satisfy themselves that this is true. Have them embrace each other out of joy; and do not forget their prayer of thanksgiving.

*d.* Conclude by showing that the manna fell every day, to make them strong in their journey. Remind the children that God is caring for them as he cared for the Israelites long ago.

## Dramatization.

*Three boys play the characters.*

*(Enter three Israelites L.)*

FIRST: I do not think I can live another day. I am very weak.

SECOND: Yes, and some of our people are weaker than we are.

THIRD: The boys and girls will all die if we do not get something to eat soon.

SECOND: We have all asked God to help us.

FIRST: Yes, we have all prayed to Him.

THIRD: We have been praying for many days.

FIRST : What is this ? *(Reaches out hand)*     It is hail. We are going to have a storm.

SECOND : It is good that we are near home. We have not far to go.

THIRD : The storm will give colds to our boys and girls. They are so weak that many of them will die.

SECOND : What is that cry? Some one said food. They are eating the hail.

FIRST : Yes, they are. We must eat some.

*(All stoop down and pick up a piece of imaginary manna.)*

SECOND : It is bread.

THIRD : It is very good bread.

FIRST : I never ate such good bread.

THIRD : We must go to our home and get a dish in which to put it.

SECOND : But first we must thank God.

FIRST : Yes, we must tell Him we thank Him for this good bread.

*(All kneel in silence)*

**Silent Reading.** *Gathering Bread.*

Before reading the story in class, divide the class into two groups. Tell the children that there are many loaves of different kinds of bread in the story. They must gather them. The words are the different kinds of bread, and the number of times they occur is the number of loaves of that kind of bread in the story. The child that first gives the correct number of times each word occurs scores a point for his group. Suggested words in this story, with the number of times each occurs. :

to—9; God—5; they—4; home—3; bread—3;
down—3; came—3; he—3.

### Related Stories from Other Sources.

An angel of the Lord fed Elias with bread and water in his exile (III Kings, xix, 4-8).

St. Paschal Baylon (May 17), a Franciscan, had a special devotion to the Blessed Sacrament. He would spend hours on his knees before the tabernacle. On one occasion, while he was still a shepherd boy, he heard the consecration bell ring in the church in the valley below the hill where he was tending sheep. He fell to his knees, when suddenly there stood before him an angel bearing in his hands the Sacred Host, and offering it for Paschal's adoration.

"King Alfred and the Beggar" ("Fifty Famous Stories Retold," Baldwin) shows how in return for Alfred's denial of himself to help a beggar, his men were rewarded with a great draught of fishes, and he himself was given victory over the Danes.

### A BAD BOY (138)

Frank was a bad boy. He took eggs from the robins. His mother said he should not do it. One day Frank saw the home of some robins. It was up in a tree. He went up into the tree. The wind went blowing around the tree. Frank did not hear it. He was thinking about the eggs. As he was taking the eggs, he fell. The wind made him fall. He said he would never take eggs from the robins again. If we ask Him, Jesus will be like the wind. He will keep away any bad boy or girl who wants to take us from Him.

### Related Stories in "Teacher Tells a Story."

This story should be followed by story 142.

### Development of "A Bad Boy."

*a.* Ask the children if they have ever heard the wind whistle about their homes on a cold winter's night. If possible, have one of them imitate it for you. If they will not respond, you must try to imitate it yourself. Personify the wind, make it desire to be inside the house, enjoying the heat of the fire, and listening to the stories that daddy or mother is telling. Have it say to itself in resignation that perhaps it is too rough to be admitted inside. You may become humorous by having the wind reflect upon some ludicrous things it might do once it were in the house, for instance, it might blow the table cloth over the chandelier, and put the carpet on the table.

*b.* Note, however, that the wind is strong; and that it is obedient to God. When it blows, it is doing the work that God gave it to do. Say that you know of a good deed the wind did for some robin friends of yours. Think aloud and ask yourself whether the children would like to hear about it. Make up your mind to tell them, if they will be attentive. The way is now open for the story itself.

*c.* Make something of the temptation that came to Frank when he saw the robin's nest. Make him remember his mother's words. Have him start towards the tree several times, and as many times retrace his steps. Finally, however, he surrenders.

*d.* Tell how the wind commenced to hum angrily as soon as Frank surrendered. Imitate its humming, and its gradually growing growl. At various heights in Frank's climb, bring in the wind; and note Frank's inattention to it. As he gets nearer and nearer the eggs, make the wind howl louder than ever. Make his reach just a little too short. As he stretches, have him fall, blown from his position by the wind.

*e.* Show that Our Lord guards us, as the wind guarded the robin's nest.

**Dramatization.**

*Three characters: Frank, Frank's mother, the doctor.
(Frank's arm is in a sling.)*

DOCTOR: Well, Frank, now that I am through, how did it happen?

FRANK: O doctor! I feel too sick to tell you now.

MOTHER: He says that he was climbing a tree for a robin's nest.

DOCTOR: Were you?

FRANK: Yes, but I will never do it again.

MOTHER: I told him not to go up into trees.

FRANK: I did not want to go.

MOTHER: Well why did you go?

FRANK: The devil asked me to go.

MOTHER: And you did what he told you?

FRANK: But I will never do it again.

MOTHER: And it was the wind that made him fall.

DOCTOR: Oh! I see! The wind was good to the robins.

FRANK: Yes, Doctor, the wind made me fall. I am glad it did. I should never do what mother said, if it had not. Now I will always do what she tells me.

DOCTOR: I am glad to hear that, Frank. I shall ask your mother sometimes if you are doing what she wants.

FRANK: You will always hear her say yes to that, Doctor.

DOCTOR: Well, I must see some other sick people. I think you should go to bed for the rest of the day, Frank. Good-by.

FRANK and MOTHER: Good-by.
                    *(Doctor exits L.)*

MOTHER: Come, Frank, you heard what the Doctor said.

FRANK: Yes, and I want to do what you tell me.
                    *(Exeunt both R.)*

**Silent Reading.** *Correcting Mistakes.*

Before the story is read in class, divide the class into two groups. Have children read one sentence at a time. After a minute or two, according to length of sentence, tell them to close their books. Then express that sentence with an error in it, for instance, express sentence 2: "He took *the nest* from the robins." Ask the children if the sentence is correct; and if it is not, they are to tell you where the error is. The first to detect the error scores a point for his group. This exercise is meant to develop the critical faculty and to encourage exactness in the children's own reading.

**Related Stories from Other Sources.**

Jeremias foretells a pestilential wind as a punishment for Babylon because of its afflicting the Israelites (Jeremias, li, 1–12).

St. Felix of Valois (November 20) one of the founders of the Order of the Holy Trinity, was moved to this step by a desire to free Christian captives from the power which had stolen them from their homes.

St. Cornelius (September 16), Pope, was zealous in bringing back to the true fold those who had been robbed of their faith by the persecution of Decius.

"The Ungrateful Guest" ("Fifty Famous Stories Retold," Baldwin) tells how King Philip of Macedon had burned on the forehead of one who robbed his own host the words, "The Ungrateful Guest," in punishment for his crime.

The value of the wind to men can be found in the story, "The Wind's Work" ("Mother Stories," Lindsay).

**PLAYFUL TOWSER (139)**

Towser was a little dog. He was very old. But if he should run at you, you would get away from him. Towser lived with

Mrs. Leroy. One day a little girl and her mother were at the home of Mrs. Leroy. When all were playing, Towser thought he would play, too. So he ran at this little girl. Towser was having a good time, because she ran away. Do you know where she ran? She ran to her mother. Towser did not run after her any more. He thought Mrs. Leroy would hit him. She made him leave the room. He did not like that, but he had to go. Jesus wants us to run away from sin to Him.

### Related Stories in "Teacher Tells a Story."

This story should be followed by stories 140, 141, and 143–145, inclusive.

### Development of "Playful Towser."

*a.* Ask the children if they have ever been frightened by another child who deliberately caused their fright for his own amusement. In order to bring home clearly the question, show that on Hallowe'en bad boys sometimes put on sheets and stand in dark places, so that they can jump out and shout, "Boo!" when some child passes. Allow the children to relate their experiences in this matter, if they have had any. Condemn the children who perform these tricks; note that sometimes children are so badly frightened that they die from the shock.

*b.* Remark that you know a little dog who was rightly punished for frightening a little girl. Say that he was no more a vicious dog, than a boy in a sheet is a ghost. But add that the little girl did not know how old he was, nor that he had no teeth.

*c.* Enter into the thoughts of Towser as he contemplates frightening the child. Make his reflections humorous, as he forecasts what she may do in her fright; make him think how much fun it would be if she hung on to the chandelier, or crawled into the Victrola. Add that Mrs. Leroy was thinking other thoughts, namely, where she would put Towser, if he frightened anyone that day.

*d.* While Towser is chasing the little girl, make him laugh to himself at her terror. Show his disappointment when she runs to her mother. Make much of the mother's protecting power.

*e.* Ask the children whether they think Towser ought to be punished. Estimate their moral reaction by asking why they think so.

*f.* Do not forget to insist upon the protecting power of Jesus, who will disappoint the devil, if we run to Him.

**Dramatization.**

*Three characters, Mrs. Leroy, the little girl, and her mother.*

*(All three are seated).*

MOTHER: How are you now, dear?

GIRL: I feel much better now.

MRS. LEROY: Towser was only playing. But this will teach him not to play that way again.

MOTHER: I am glad you sent him out of the room.

MRS. LEROY: But he could not hurt anyone.

GIRL: He couldn't. How is that?

MRS. LEROY: He is too old. He can not bite.

GIRL: If I had known that, I would not have run.

MRS. LEROY: I was glad to see you run to your mother. Towser did not run after you, when he saw where you were going.

GIRL: I always go to mother for help. I know she will not let me be hurt.

MOTHER: But, when the devil is running after you, to whom do you run.

GIRL: I run to Jesus.

MRS. LEROY: And does He help you as mother does?

GIRL: Yes, He always makes the devil run away. It is easy to do what God wants when I ask Jesus to help me.

MRS. LEROY: I am glad that you love Jesus so much. I know that you and your mother will be glad to go to see Him with me.

GIRL: When are you going?

MRS. LEROY: I will go now, if you will come with me.

GIRL and MOTHER: We shall be glad to go.

MRS. LEROY: Come along, then.

*(Exeunt all, R.)*

**Silent Reading.** *Want Ads.*

Before the story is read in class, divide the class into two groups. Have a newspaper on your desk, and say that there are ads in the paper asking for answers to various questions. Say that the answers are in the story. Permit the children to hunt through the story for the answer. The child that first answers correctly scores a point for his group.

Suggested questions are:

What was Towser? Where did Towser live? Was Towser old?

How old was Towser? Would you get away from him?

Who were at the home of Mrs. Leroy?

Did Towser run at the little girl?

To whom did the little girl run?

Was Towser having a good time?

Why was Towser having a good time?

What does Jesus want you to do?

What did Mrs. Leroy make Towser do?

## Related Stories from Other Sources.

Mary Magdalen ran from temptation to the feet of Jesus and bathed them with her tears (St. Matthew, xxvi, 6-13).

St. Camillus de Lellis (July 18) acted as rescuer of the sick, devoting all his energy to their physical and spiritual comfort. He was the founder of an order devoted to the care of the sick.

St. Jerome Emilian (July 20) protected the orphans from the pangs of hunger, and from disease; but also from the temptations that lack of religious training would have cast in their way.

The Sisters of Charity protected the soldiers on the battlefield at Gettysburg, both from the death that their wounds might have caused, and from unrepentant death in the case of those whose wounds would not respond to their patient nursing.

"About Angels" (in "Golden Windows," Richards) shows that a mother is ready to protect her child, when others neglect it.

### TRIXIE IN TROUBLE (156)

Madeline had a little dog. She called him Trixie. Trixie was a bad little dog. He would bite at other dogs. Madeline told him not to do that. The very next day he did the same thing. He saw a big dog going by the house. Trixie ran at him, as if to bite him. The big dog ran at Trixie, and did bite him. Trixie ran crying into the house. Madeline was going to hit him. She took care of him, when she saw the bite. Soon Trixie was well again. Sin is like the big dog. It will bite us if we try to play with it. The bite of sin is taken away by the priest when we tell him our sins.

## Related Stories in "Teacher Tells a Story."

This story should be preceded by stories 146–155, inclusive; and followed by stories 166–172, inclusive.

## Development of "Trixie in Trouble."

*a.* Ask the children if any of them has a little dog at home. Have one of them describe his pet, if you can. If not describe one yourself. Make Trixie resemble either one of these dogs that have been spoken of. Note particularly that he is a little dog.

*b.* Say that there are some small children who like to annoy larger ones. They do this because they think the larger children will not hurt them, and because they enjoy themselves doing it. Think aloud and say that it is a poor kind of enjoyment. Reflect and say you think none of your class would make others uncomfortable, just for his own fun.

*c.* Commence the story of Trixie, remarking that he was like these small children who annoy the larger. Enter into Trixie's mind as he sees the large dog coming along. Have him say to himself that Madeline was too careful of him; that he was never hurt before. Have him anticipate the annoyance he will cause the large dog, and laugh to himself over the surprise he will cause. Make him look around so that he will have a free course in his flight after he has snapped at the large dog.

*d.* Show how his expectations were frustrated; he does not have the enjoyment he expected, he does not have an opportunity to run away, and he is badly injured.

*e.* Make his crying ludicrous by saying that one would think Trixie was trying to tell all his dog friends in the world that he was hurt, or in some other way.

*f.* Insist on Madeline's first impulse; show that she felt like punishing him; have her in the act of striking him, until she sees the wound. Then describe forcibly the patience she manifested in caring for it.

Make her shed a tear or two over the wound. When she has cared for it, have her ask Trixie if he means to do the same thing again. Have him shake his head no, and note that Madeline thought she saw him drop a tear.

**Dramatization.**

*Two characters: Madeline and her mother.*

MOTHER: I heard Trixie crying, but I did not know what was wrong.

MADELINE: Oh! he was biting at big dogs again.

MOTHER: Did one of them bite back?

MADELINE: Yes, and hurt Trixie, too.

MOTHER: Do you think he will be well again?

MADELINE: Yes, mother. I have taken good care of him.

MOTHER: He will soon be hurt again, I think.

MADELINE: What do you mean, mother?

MOTHER: I mean that he will soon be biting at big dogs again.

MADELINE: No, he will not.

MOTHER: What makes you think so?

MADELINE: I asked him, after I had taken care of him.

MOTHER: But a dog can not talk.

MADELINE: No, but a dog can cry. And I saw a tear come from Trixie's eye. And when I wanted to know if he would bite at big dogs again, he nodded no.

MOTHER: I hope he will not. He might die the next time.

MADELINE: I know, mother, he means what he says. But, mother, won't you come and see how well I have cared for him?

MOTHER: Yes, Madeline, I will. Where is he?

MADELINE: *(pointing L.)* He is out in his own house, on a new bed of straw.

*(Exeunt both L.)*

**Silent Reading.** *Fast Trains.*

Before the story is read in class, the teacher tells the pupils they are trains, and the words in the story are miles. Teacher wants to know which of the children can travel the greatest number of miles in a minute. They commence reading silently when teacher says, "Go." And they stop, when she calls, "Time," marking the place, and counting the number of words they have read. The fastest train is he who has read the greatest number of words, and at the same time is able to give the meaning of the sentences in which they stand.

**Related Stories from Other Sources.**

St. Peter ran into temptation by going among the enemies of Our Lord, who accused him of being Christ's friend. He denied it three times. But then went out and wept bitter tears, and was reconciled with Our Lord through his repentance (St. Matthew, xxvi, 70–75).

St. Afra (August 7), a sinner, was taken prisoner as a Christian and ordered to offer sacrifice to idols. She had faith in Christ, though she had not lived up to it throughout her life, and refused to offend Him by idolatry. Her conversion was sincere. She died at the stake for Christ.

St. Margaret of Cortona (February 22) left her father's home to disobey God. She went into the occasion of sin, and sin overcame her. But she came back to her father after ten years, and did public penance in her parish church. So sincere was her repent-

ance that she continually mortified herself lest she go
again into the occasion of sin.

A striking example of reconciliation is that of England's surrender to the obedience of the Pope under
the daughter of Henry VIII, Queen Mary.

Comparable to Madeline's care for Trixie is that of
Androclus for the lion, in "Androclus and the Lion"
("Fifty Famous Stories Retold," Baldwin).

### THE RUNAWAY LAMB (157)

Once in a field there were many lambs. One of the lambs did
not want to be where the others were. He would not do what
his mother said. One day he ran away as far as he could go.
He was running so fast, he did not see the hole in his way.
He fell into the hole. But a man took care of the lambs. He
saw that the lamb had run away. He ran after him. He took
the lamb back home. The lamb never ran away again. The
bad boy and girl are like this lamb. The priest goes after the
bad boy and girl. He wants to keep them away from sin.

## Related Stories in "Teacher Tells a Story."

This story should be preceded by stories 146–156, inclusive, and followed by stories 166–172.

## Development of "The Runaway Lamb."

a. Create interest by asking the children if they have
any woolen garments, mittens, sweaters, or overcoats.
Tell them that these are made by machines from the
hair of sheep. Describe as well as you can the shear-
ing and the process of manufacture. A very elaborate
description will not be necessary. The point is to make
the children take somewhat of a personal interest in
the characters in the story.

b. Say that young sheep are called lambs, and that
they must be obedient to the mother sheep, or they
would all die or be killed before they would grow to be

sheep. The result would be that after a little while we should have no more wool. Say that you know a story which shows how dangerous it is for lambs to disobey the mother sheep.

*c.* Enter into the story. Show the lamb fretting about his confinement; make his imagination work, and see all kinds of wonderful pastures where he might run just as he pleased; make him complain of his mother, of the shepherd, and of the other sheep and lambs.

*d.* Represent him as trying to run away several times previous to the accident; but show that each time he was caught before anything happened to him. Let the mother chastise him on each occasion; but have him fret all the more.

*e.* Develop gradually the opportunity for the disastrous runaway. First have the shepherd's attention called to another part of the flock, where one of the sheep has been injured; then show the mother interested in something passing in the road; have the lamb wander quietly to the outer edge of the flock, and then commence to run.

*f.* Show his heightening joy as he realizes he is free, and bring it to its height just as he falls into the pit. Have him show bewilderment at first; then sorrow, first for his plight, and as the time lengthens, for disobedience.

*g.* Create suspense by showing that the shepherd hesitates about going after the lamb. He is disgusted. The lamb has tried his patience. After several resolves not to follow the lamb, have him make up his mind to search for him once more.

*h.* Show the lamb's anticipation when he hears the approach of the shepherd; have him lick the shepherd's hand; when he is taken back to the flock, make him lick his mother's face.   Show that in his heart is real amendment.

*i.* Approve the kindness of the shepherd, and show how the priest is like him.

**Dramatization.**

*Characters: two shepherds.*

*(Enter both L.)*

FIRST SHEPHERD: I almost lost a lamb today.

SECOND: Why, how was that?

FIRST: It was the same one that ran away before.

SECOND: Did he run away again?

FIRST: Yes, while I was caring for one of the sheep.

SECOND: Did you go after him?

FIRST: Yes, I did.

SECOND: I thought you said you would not go after him again.

FIRST: I did say that.

SECOND: Well, why did you go after him?

FIRST: Because I love him.

SECOND: Love a bad little lamb?

FIRST: Yes, and you love all your lambs, too.

SECOND: But all mine are good.

FIRST: But if you had a bad one, you would love him.   I was going to let the lamb stay away, this time.   But I am glad I went after him.

SECOND: Why?

FIRST: He fell into a hole.

SECOND: And would have died there.

FIRST: Yes, if I had not found him.

SECOND: Will he live?

FIRST: Yes, I have taken good care of him, since I found him.

SECOND: Will he run away again?

FIRST: No, I think he will not. He licked my hand, and licked his mother's face, as if to say he was glad he was back, and would not run away again.

*(Both walk slowly to R. E.)*

SECOND: *(talking as he walks)* I am glad that you went after him. It will teach all the other lambs not to run away.

FIRST: Yes, when he tells them about the hole, they will all want to stay with me.

*(Exeunt).*

**Silent Reading.** *The Sign Posts.*

Before the story is read in class, divide the class into two groups. Tell the children that they are travelers, and that the sentences are signs at cross roads. Ask the children to read the signs one at a time, and tell what they say. The child that first gives correctly the meaning of the sentence scores a point for his group.

**Related Stories from Other Sources.**

True repentance is found in the case of David, who recognized his sin when admonished by Nathan (acting as the shepherd), and did penance with a firm purpose of amendment (II Kings, xii, 1–13).

St. Nonnus acted as the shepherd in the case of St. Pelagia, penitent (October 8). A sermon of his recalled her to penance while she was in the snares of the devil. After four years of austere penance, she died, faithful to her penitential resolve.

It was the mother of St. Andrew Corsini (February 4), who acted as the reclaiming shepherd for him. In the midst of his sins she reproached him, told him that God had sent him to her in answer to her prayers, and that she had vowed him to God. She related a dream she had before he was born, in which she saw her son as a wolf rush into a church, and become a lamb. It was this talk of his mother's that recalled him to the penance that made of him a saint.

### THE SORRY CHICK (158)

"Do not go so close to the water," a mother hen said to her little chick. She thought it might fall in. The chick said that it would not go close to the water again. But it wanted to see itself in the water. So it went close to the water again. This time it fell in. A little girl saw it fall. She took it out of the water. The chick never went close to the pond again. Sin is like a pond for us. If we fall into it, some one must take us out. The priest will do this for those who do not want to go near sin again. He will do it when we tell him our sins.

## Related Stories in "Teacher Tells a Story."

This story should be preceded by stories 146–157, inclusive; and followed by stories 159–172, inclusive. Other stories of similar thought matter are: 60–63.

## Development of "The Sorry Chick."

*a.* Ask the children if they have ever used a basin of water for a mirror to view their faces. If any child wants to speak of his experiences in this way, permit him to do so. Then reflect that a bowl of water is not a very good mirror; but add that little chicks have no other. Say it is not surprising that they should make use of a bowl of water, or of a pond of water in which to view themselves.

*b.* Show how the sorry chick wanted to see itself in a pond. Bring out forcibly the folly of vanity; remark that probably it wanted to see how much prettier it was than the other chicks. Lament the fact that vanity usually brings disaster.

*c.* Have the mother become very much excited when she sees the chick so near the pond; humorously describe the speed with which she flew to the side of the chick, and pulled it away from the pond with her beak; make much of her chastisement.

*d.* Regret aloud the power of vanity. Show that it brought the chick back to the pond again. Describe the chick's leaning nearer and nearer the water, remarking to itself that it must have a better view of itself, and that it is perfectly safe. Note the slipping of the ground under the feet of the chick, which the chick does not notice, and then suddenly the splash, and the chick is in the pond, frightened and about to drown.

*e.* Have the mother see the chick fall in, describe her excitement, show that she becomes quieter as the little girl goes to the rescue. When the chick is taken out of the pond, the mother makes up her mind to punish it well. But when she sees its contrite look, she forgives it. Insist upon the genuine character of the chick's resolve not to go near the pond again, and its consequent struggle to overcome its vanity.

**Dramatization.**

*Two characters: a little girl and her mother.*

*(Enter both L.)*

GIRL: I saved a life today, mother.

MOTHER: You did? How?

GIRL: I saved someone from sinking.

MOTHER: Whom could you save? You are not strong enough.

GIRL: I saved a little chick.

MOTHER: How did it fall into the water?

GIRL: It was trying to see itself in the water.

MOTHER: I thought the mother hen would tell it to stay away from it.

GIRL: I think she did. I saw her pull it away once.

MOTHER: So, the chick would not do what its mother told it.

GIRL: No, it came back again. And then fell in.

MOTHER: If it had done what its mother said, it would not have fallen in.

GIRL: It is a good thing I was there. The chick would be dead now, if I had not been.

MOTHER: What did the mother hen do when you saved the chick?

GIRL: I thought she was going to peck at it. But the chick looked very sorry, and she took it under her wing, to dry it.

MOTHER: Do you think the chick will go near the pond again?

GIRL: No, I think not. I think it knows better, now. And I, too, know that I must do what you say, or something bad will happen to me.

MOTHER: I am glad to hear that. Come and tell it to your daddy, too.

*(Exeunt both R.)*

**Silent Reading.** *Playing Soldier.*

Have the children read silently a sentence, then close their books. Write the words of the sentence in a changed order upon the blackboard. The child that names the word that stands first in the sentence in the book is made general of that army; the others who name the succeeding words in correct order become his soldiers. The succeeding sentences should be read in a similar way. The purpose of the exercise is to aid in sentence composition, and in faithful reporting of matter read.

## Related Stories from Other Sources.

God revoked the sentence of destruction against Nineve upon the repentance of its inhabitants following the preaching of Jonas (Jonas, iii).

St. Fidelis of Sigmaringen (April 24) suffered martyrdom at the hands of the Calvinists in Switzerland in his attempt to lift them out of their heresy.

"The Fox and the Goat" (Aesop's Fables) brings out the danger of leaping without looking whither one is going. The goat leaps into a well that was too deep to permit his getting out again, and that at the advice of the fox, who had fallen in and saw that the goat could help him out, if the former should come into the well, too.

### LAWRENCE AND HIS SISTER (174)

Lawrence did many things his sister did not like. He said many things to make her cry. One day he told another boy that he would not do this any more. The other boy was glad. He thought Lawrence was going to be a good boy. But Lawrence told him he was not going to do it because his mother always hit him for it. He never thought that God loved his sister. The other boy asked him why he did not love his sister. He said that Lawrence should love her because God does. He should love her because God wants him to.

## Related Stories in "Teacher Tells a Story."

This story should be preceded by stories 172 and 173.

## Development of "Lawrence and His Sister."

*a.* Describe the home at Nazareth; show how quiet everything was there. Reflect that you would have been delighted to live there. Ask rhetorically if the children would not like to make their homes as peaceful as the home where Our Lord lived.   Be shocked at the quarreling that goes on in some homes.

*b.* Say that you know a story of a little boy who was always making his home a disagreeable place in which to live.  Ask the children if they would like to hear the story.  Upon their assurance that they would, go on with the story as it is found in the book.

*c.* Show how trivial are most of the quarrels among children, over a cooky, or the relative size of apples given them, or carrying tales.

*d.* Enter into Lawrence's mind as he makes the resolution not to quarrel with his sister again.  Show the spitefulness and bitterness that rankles there.  Show that he makes the resolution grudgingly, but from a sense of expediency.

*e.* Have the good boy use great persuasion in bringing Lawrence around to his point of view; make Lawrence unwilling to see it at first, let him bring objections that are answered; finally show the victory in which Lawrence adopts the higher motive for his resolution.

**Dramatization.**

*Characters: Lawrence and his boy friend.*

*(Enter both R.)*

LAWRENCE: No, sir, I will not fight with her again.

FRIEND: Oh! how glad I am to hear you say that.

LAWRENCE: Why?  Do you think my sister and I are friends now?

FRIEND: Yes, aren't you?

LAWRENCE: We are not and we never shall be.

FRIEND: Do not say that.  You must love your sister.

LAWRENCE: Love her?  Ha! ha! ha!

FRIEND: Why did you make up your mind not to fight?

LAWRENCE: Because when I hit her, mother hits me.

FRIEND: And you don't want your mother to hit you again.

LAWRENCE: That's right.

FRIEND: Why?

LAWRENCE: Say, don't ask me why I don't want mother to hit me. Don't you know it hurts?

FRIEND: Of course I do. Why don't you think of that when you hit your sister?

LAWRENCE: I do. She ought to be hurt.

FRIEND: Don't you know that God loves your sister?

LAWRENCE: I can't love her.

FRIEND: Well, then, you can't love God.

LAWRENCE: Yes, I can. God knows that she treats me mean.

FRIEND: But even if He does, He wants you to love her. Don't you remember how He prayed for the Jews who put Him on the cross?

LAWRENCE: That's right, He did.

FRIEND: And your sister has never done that to you.

LAWRENCE: No, nothing nearly so bad.

FRIEND: Can't you pray for her, then?

LAWRENCE: It's going to be hard, but I can do it.

FRIEND: Shake hands on that. *(They shake hands and walk towards L. E.)* You'll find after a little while that your sister is better than you think she is.

*(Exeunt both).*

**Silent Reading.** *The Angels.*

After the story is read in class, divide the class into two groups. All books are to be closed. Write questions about the story on the blackboard. These questions are angels that have come to see how well the children have read. The child that first answers each question correctly, scores a point for his group.

Suggested questions for this story:

What kind of things did Lawrence do?
What kind of things did he say?
What did he tell the other boy?
Was the other boy glad to hear that?
Why was the other boy glad?
Why was Lawrence going to stop doing bad things?
Did Lawrence think that God loved his sister?
What did the other boy ask Lawrence?
Did the other boy tell Lawrence why he should love his sister?
Why should Lawrence love his sister?

### Related Stories from Other Sources.

The repentance of King Antiochus in his last illness was not accepted because it was not genuine (II Macchabees, ix).

The zeal of Lawrence's friend may be associated with the apostolic spirit of St. John Francis Regis (June 16) who on one occasion was struck in the face by a sinner. The saint said to him, "If you only knew me, you would give me more than that." On another occasion he went into the confessional to hear confessions after he had broken his leg, and without any surgical attention. After several hours, the leg was found to be miraculously healed.

The friendly reunion of North and South after the Civil War may be brought forth as an example of what true reconciliation should be; and the peace now existing between them, as typical of the peace that should characterize brothers and sisters.

"The Cooky" (in "Golden Windows," Richards) shows an angel rebuking a child for making a cooky his brother by loving it more than his natural brother, whom he is beating in order to gain possession of the food.

"Why the White Hares Have Black Ears" ("The Book of Nature Myths," Holbrook) shows the spirit of the forest beating the ears of the white hares with a firebrand till their ears are black, because they were quarrelsome.

### WHY HE GOES TO MASS (175)

"I'm going to Mass every Sunday after this," said Michael. "Sister makes us stay in after school, when we do not go to Mass. I want to go home when the other boys and girls go." "Is that why you are going to Mass?" asked his friend. "Don't you know that God wants you to go to Mass? If you do not go, He is sad. You know He is in His house for you. And he would like you to go to see Him every day. But on Sunday, when you will not go, you hurt God. You tell Him you are not going to do what He wants." Michael said he would go to Mass every Sunday, because God wanted him to go.

### Related Stories in "Teacher Tells a Story."

This story should be preceded by stories 173 and 174; and followed by stories 176–178.

### Development of "Why He Goes to Mass."

a. Ask the children what they do when they go home after school. Call on one to tell what his particular work is. Ask him if he would like to stay in and do some school work after the other children went home. Ask his reason, if he says he would not want to stay.

b. Say that you heard about a little boy who had to

stay in after the other children went home nearly every Monday. Ask yourself why it was always Monday rather than some other day. Ask the children if they can guess why it was Monday on which he was punished.

*c.* If they can not guess, tell them it was because he missed Mass the day before. Say that he became impatient of staying in after the other children. Enter into the thoughts of the boy; have him blame everybody but himself for his punishment; show that he finally decides to go to Mass every Sunday so that he will not be obliged to remain in school on Mondays.

*d.* Have Michael communicate this resolution and the reason for it to his friend. Show his friend persuading him to change his motive. Do not allow Michael to agree too quickly with his friend. Rapid conversions are miracles. Have Michael question God's being hurt because one boy stays away; have him object that God would let him off on the Sundays when he is too tired to get up. Make his friend answer his objections. Then gradually bring Michael around to his point of view.

**Dramatization.**

*Two characters: Michael and his Friend.*

*(Enter both R.)*

MICHAEL: Yes, I am going to Mass every Sunday after this.

FRIEND: I am glad to hear that.

MICHAEL: I do not want to stay in school on Mondays after the other boys and girls go.

FRIEND: No, I wouldn't either.

MICHAEL: And Sister makes every one stay in on Monday who does not go to Mass on Sunday.

FRIEND: Is that why you are going to Mass?

MICHAEL: Yes.

FRIEND: Don't you know that God wants you to go to Mass?

MICHAEL: I know He wants me to go sometimes.

FRIEND: He wants you to go every Sunday.

MICHAEL: Even when I am tired?

FRIEND: Yes, even then. And God is hurt when you do not go.

MICHAEL: He is hurt when one little boy stays away?

FRIEND: Yes, because He loves you even if you are little.

MICHAEL: And does He feel sad when I will not go to Mass?

FRIEND: Yes, and He is hoping that you will do what He asks.

MICHAEL: Well, if He looks after me like that, I ought to do what He asks.

FRIEND: You are going to Mass then to please Him?

MICHAEL: Yes.

FRIEND: And not because you do not want to stay in?

MICHAEL: I would go even if I did not have to stay in when I missed Mass.

FRIEND: I am glad to hear you talk that way. *(Both walk towards L. E.)* And I know God is glad, too.

*(Exeunt both).*

**Silent Reading.** *Gathering Sea Shells.*

After reading the lesson in class, divide the class into two groups. Tell them they are to go along the seashore, which is their lesson, and pick up all the shells they can of a given kind. The different words are different kinds of shell. The child that first finds the correct number of times a given word occurs in the story scores a point for his group.

Suggested words for this story:

> to—11; go—9; Mass—5; he—5; Sunday—3; going—3; God—3; is—3.

### Related Stories from Other Sources.

Compare the entering the church for Mass at God's wish to Noe's entering the ark at God's command (Genesis, vi and vii).

St. Philip Neri (May 26) wished his disciples to serve God, like the first Christians, in gladness of heart. He said it was this that gave the soul greater power over temptation, and fuller aid to perseverance.

St. John Chrysostom (January 27), Bishop of Constantinople, was very urgent upon the point of frequent attendance at the Holy Sacrifice by the members of his flock; in order to remove all excuse, he abbreviated the long liturgy until then in use.

Duke Henry of Silesia, the son of St. Hedwig, assisted at the Holy Sacrifice before entering the battle in which he was killed.

The self-interest displayed by Michael in the beginning is illustrated in the fable, "The Peasant and the Apple Tree" (Aesop's Fables) in which a peasant, unmoved by the entreaties of grasshoppers and sparrows that beg him to spare the tree, finally leaves it stand when he discovers that bees make their home there and that he can gather the honey they make.

### MARTIN'S GOOD FRIEND (176)

"Come on, we will get something to eat." This is what Martin said to his friend. He wanted his friend to take what was not his. He did not want him to pay for what he was going to take. "I will not take what is not mine." This is what his friend said. "If your father gave your brother something to eat, would you take it from him while your father was looking? God gives boys and girls every thing they have. He does not want others to take these things from them. He looks to see if any one does so. I am not going to do what you ask. God would see me, if I did."

### Related Stories in "Teacher Tells a Story."

This story should be preceded by stories 173–175; and followed by stories 177 and 178.

### Development of "Martin's Good Friend."

*a.* Ask the children if they pass any fruit stores on their way to school. Have one of them, if possible, describe the various fruits he has observed on the stand in front of the store, or in the window. If this fails, make the necessary description yourself. Note humorously that bad boys seem to think that because the owner of the store puts the fruit out in front, he does not want it. Add that if the owner caught these boys stealing, he would show them whether he wanted the fruit or not. Say something about the policeman, jail, and the like.

*b.* Say that bad boys who steal often try to make others steal, too. Say you heard about one that tried to do that. Ask the children if they would like to hear whether or not he made the other boy steal.

*c.* Tell of the two boys walking along to school, when Martin sees the fruit stand. Say that the owner was in front of the store, and Martin asked his friend to stop until the man went inside. Then when the owner has gone inside, Martin makes the proposition in haste. When his friend refuses, have Martin misunderstand his motives. Have him say the fruit is good; make him protest that the owner is too old to run; have him assure his friend that there are no policemen about.

*d.* Then dramatically his friend says that Martin has forgotten some one whom they must fear more than the policeman. Do not say who this is until the end. This will maintain suspense.

*e.* Martin's friend makes the argument from stealing from one's brother in the presence of one's father. He asks if Martin knows who gave the owner of the store the fruit. Martin hesitates, but finally gives the correct answer. Then his friend says that God is the Father of all; that He is looking down upon all; and that they can not steal the fruit without God's seeing them. He adds that Martin may steal, if he likes; as for him, he will not. Martin sheepishly agrees with him, and refuses to steal, and they both continue on their way to school.

## Dramatization.

*Two characters: Martin and his friend.*

*(Enter both R.)*

MARTIN : Let's wait here a moment.

FRIEND : We shall be late for school.

MARTIN : Come on, now we can go. Come on and get something to eat.

FRIEND : Where?

MARTIN : Over there.

FRIEND : Who is going to pay?

MARTIN : We will not pay, we will just take.

FRIEND : I will not do it.

MARTIN : Come on, the things are good to eat.

FRIEND : No.

MARTIN : The man is too old to run.

FRIEND : I will not go.

MARTIN : And there is no policeman here.

FRIEND : But there is someone looking.

MARTIN : Who is it ?

FRIEND : Who gave the things to that man ?

MARTIN : I do not know.

FRIEND : You do. Who gives us all that we have ?

MARTIN : God ?

FRIEND : Yes. Would you take from your brother something your father gave him, while your father was looking ?

MARTIN : No.

FRIEND : Well, God would see us take from that man what He gave him. I will not do it. You may, if you wish.

MARTIN : Let's go. I don't want to do it, either.

*(Exeunt both L.)*

**Silent Reading.** *Jumping Fences.*

Before the story is read in class, divide the class into two groups. Tell them that you are going to jump fences. The even sentences will be the fences. Read the odd sentences in class, and after reading the third, have the second read silently. Call that going back to look at the fence. Ask for a description of the fence (the meaning of the sentence). The child that first gives the correct meaning scores a point for his side. Skip the fourth, read the fifth in class, then have the fourth read silently, and so on.

**Related Stories from Other Sources.**

The Israelites were punished with temporary defeat because one of them, Achan, took of the things forbidden the Israelites by God. After Achan was punished by being stoned to death, victory once more came to the Jews (Joshua, vii).

Judas had been accustomed to steal the money belonging to the apostles (John, xii, 6). Suggest that this sin paved the way for his supreme crime with its appalling consequences.

St. Antoninus (May 10), Dominican, and Archbishop of Florence, showed the virtue opposed to the greed that prompts dishonesty. His goods were always at the service of the poor, and frequently he had not in his house the very necessities of life.

Francis Bacon, Lord Chancellor of England (1618), used his office to enrich himself by taking bribes. As a result, he was deprived of his office, fined heavily, and sentenced to prison during the King's pleasure.

"The Pied Piper of Hamelin" ("How to Tell Stories to Children," Bryant) tells how a piper who had filled his part of a contract with a mayor of a city, by leading all the rats into the sea, was refused the pay promised him, and forced justice upon the city by playing a tune that led all the children of the town after him.

## THE DUST IN THE SONG BOX (177)

Virginia had a box that could sing. Round black things were put on it to make it sing. These black things went round and round, while the box was singing. One day it did not sing very well. No one could tell why. Her father looked all over the box. He looked into it. He found too much dust where the song came out. The dust was taken away. The song of the box was good again. Her father said that sometimes what we say is like the song that was not good. God does not like it. He does not like us to tell lies. Nor to say bad words. Nor to talk about our friends. We must say only good things.

## Related Stories in "Teacher Tells a Story."

This story should be preceded by stories 173–176, inclusive; and followed by story 178.

## Development of "Dust in the Song Box."

*a.* Ask the children if they have Victrolas at home. Allow them as much self-expression on this topic as they demand. Do not permit irrelevancy, however.

*b.* Ask them if they would like to hear a story about a little girl and her Victrola. Upon their assurance that they would, commence the story as found in the book.

*c.* When you speak about the faulty reproduction, ask the children if they can tell what caused it. You may also introduce humor here by describing what the Victrola sounded like.

*d.* Prolong the inspection of the Victrola by Virginia's father. Remark that on one occasion it looked as though he were trying to climb into it. Describe the disappointment of the children in not being able to hear the music; note their growing impatience. Have the father finally find a great deal of dust lodged in the amplifier. Have him clean it out, and then test the result by playing a record. As soon as the music commences, you should tell the class that the children clapped their hands, for they knew the Victrola was all right, again.

*e.* Review the ludicrous sounds of the Victrola while the dust was in it. Ask the children if they are going to allow their voices to sound that way to God.

## Dramatization.

*Characters: Virginia and a girl friend.*

*(Enter both R.)*

VIRGINIA: Do you have a Victrola at your house?
FRIEND: Yes, we put records on it to make it sing.
VIRGINIA: Does it always sing well?
FRIEND: I think so.

VIRGINIA: You should have heard ours today.

FRIEND: What was wrong with it?

VIRGINIA: There was a lot of dust right where the song comes out.

FRIEND: Could you hear the song?

VIRGINIA: Yes, but it was so funny.     But after daddy found the dust, it was all right again.

FRIEND: I am glad to hear that.

VIRGINIA: Daddy said that what we say some times is like the song that was not good.

FRIEND: How is that?

VIRGINIA: God does not like it.

FRIEND: Oh! he means when boys and girls tell lies, or talk about their friends.

VIRGINIA: Yes, and when they say bad words.

FRIEND: Well, I am not going to sound like a dusty song box.

VIRGINIA: *(both start towards L.E.)* Nor am I.    I am going to say only good things.

## Silent Reading.  *Fruit Trees.*

Before the story is read in class, divide the class into two groups.    Tell the children that the sentences are fruit trees, and that you want them to tell you about their fruit (that is, describe what they say).    Take one sentence at a time.    The child that first gives the meaning of the sentence, scores a point for his group.

## Related Stories from Other Sources.

Aman, the adviser of King Assuerus, by evil counsel persuaded the king to issue a decree that the Jews be destroyed.    Esther, Assuerus' queen, revealed to the king the evil nature of Aman's advice, and the latter was punished by being hung on a gibbet (Esther, iii-vii).

St. Arsenius (July 19) would not speak unless obliged, and many who visited him left him without having heard him open his mouth.

"The Boy Who Cried Wolf" (Aesop's Fables) describes a shepherd boy who cried, "Wolf," so often in jest that he was not believed when a wolf really did attack the flock.

"The Fox Who Lost His Tail" (Aesop's Fables) shows how a fox who lost his tale tried by specious argument to convince the rest of his family to have their tales removed.

"The Story of Regulus" ("Fifty Famous Stories Retold," Baldwin) tells of Regulus' fidelity to his word in returning to Carthage where he knows death awaits him.

Patrick Henry, Daniel Webster, and Henry Clay may be used as examples of men who used their voices in good causes.

### A THOUGHT FOR FRIDAY (178)

"Meat will not kill you on Friday." This is what Barbara's friend said to her. Barbara said, "We know meat will not kill us on Friday. But God's priests say we are not to eat it on that day. And God wants us to do what they say. He wants us to do that because He was put on the Cross on Friday. Don't you do what your mother tells you? You do not want to make her feel sad. We do not want to make God feel sad. So we do what He wants. I never even think of meat on Friday. I knew what they did to God on Friday. I am glad to thank Him in this way."

### Related Stories in "Teacher Tells a Story."

This story should be preceded by stories 173, 177.

### Development of "A Thought for Friday."

*a.* Tell the children that on Friday the devil becomes a butcher. He carries a basket full of steaks, and sausages, and chops. He holds them out before the eyes of Catholic boys and girls, and tries to make them take some of what he offers.

*b.* Say that a little girl you know named Barbara was astonished when she found out that the devil plays butcher on Friday. She had never seen him. She was so busy doing what the priests asked her to do, that she never even felt like eating meat on Friday.

*c.* Show that Barbara's friend liked to tease her. Have the friend question her why she refuses to eat meat on Friday. When Barbara says it is to be obedient, her friend asks why it must be on Friday. This gives Barbara an opportunity to speak of the Passion. After you have told the children what Barbara said about Our Lord, think aloud and say you wish the children in your class could do the same.

## Dramatization.

*Two characters: Barbara and her friend.*

*(Enter both R.)*

FRIEND: When you come to my house on Friday you never eat meat. Why is that?

BARBARA: I am not allowed to eat meat on Friday.

FRIEND: Meat will not kill you on Friday.

BARBARA: I know it will not kill me.

FRIEND: Well, then, why don't you eat it?

BARBARA: God's priests say we are not to eat it on that day. And God wants us to do what they say.

FRIEND: Why did they pick out Friday?

BARBARA: Because Our Lord died on that day.

FRIEND: You want to show Him you love Him, is that it?

BARBARA: Yes, on the day the bad men put Him on

the Cross, we want to make ourselves suffer for Him. But really I never suffer.

FRIEND: Don't you ever feel like eating meat on Friday?

BARBARA: No, I never even think of it.

FRIEND: I could never do without it.

BARBARA: *(both start toward L.E.)* Yes, you could, if God helped you. And I am going to ask Him to-night to help you, so that you will not eat meat on Friday again.

*(Exeunt both.)*

**Silent Reading.** *The Fast Rivers.*

Before the story is read in class, divide the class into two groups. Tell the children that they are to be the rivers, and that the words in the story are trees. They must try to flow past as many trees as possible from the time you say, "Go," until you call, "Time." Then they mark the place where they stopped, and count the words they have passed. The child that has read the greatest number of words, and can tell the meaning of what he read, scores a point for his group.

**Related Stories from Other Sources.**

The Israelites murmured for flesh meat in the desert, and it was sent to them, but for their murmuring they were struck with a plague (Numbers, xi).

Some dissolute men invited St. Conrad of Piacenza (February 19) to dine with them on Friday, and had pork served to him, dressed as fish. The pork was miraculously changed into fish. After the meal the evil men accused St. Conrad of breaking the laws of the Church. St. Conrad showed them the plate full of fishbones, and the miracle worked in his behalf. This was a reward for his fasts and abstinences at other times.

### NEED FOR A LIGHT (179)

Charles could not find his top. He looked every place he thought it could be. Charles' father had a round, long, black thing that had a light in it. You could put the light on or off, just as you wanted. The father gave this light to Charles. He wanted to help find the top. After his father gave this light to him, Charles looked around many times again. Soon he found his top. When we want to tell our sins, we must know them. Some times we can not know them all, unless we have a light. The Holy Ghost has this light. If we ask Him for it, He will give it to us.

## Related Stories in "Teacher Tells a Story."

This story should be followed by stories 180–182, inclusive.

## Development of "Need for a Light."

*a.* Ask the children how many have in their homes lights that can be carried around like candles, to help you to see where you are going in the dark. Have some of the children describe its uses.

*b.* Say that it proved very useful to a boy you heard about. Tell how he lost his top. You can introduce humor by describing some of the places he looked, where it would be impossible for the top to be, in the receiver of the telephone, for instance, or in the inkwell.

*c.* Have Charles about ready to give up the search several times, only to continue it. Have him remark that if he had a light he could find it easily; make him complain that a match will not burn long enough, and besides is dangerous.

*d.* Have his father come on the scene and show interest.  Make him unwilling to let Charles have his searchlight at first; but finally after much pleading, let him give it to Charles.

*e.* Show that we do not have to plead with the Holy Ghost for light to know our sins, we need only ask Him for it.

## Dramatization.

*Two characters: Charles and his father.*

*(Enter Charles R. looking for his top).*

CHARLES: I don't know where to look for it.  I feel like giving up.  Once more, I will try.

*(Goes about stage hunting again).*

CHARLES: It looks as though I will never find it.

*(Enter Charles' father, as Charles is hunting the top).*

FATHER: What are you looking for, Charles?

CHARLES: I am looking for my top.  I need a light.

FATHER: Well, why don't you get a match?

CHARLES: A match will not burn long enough.  Besides it might start the house on fire.

FATHER: I am glad to see that you are careful.

CHARLES: I know I could find it if you would let me have your light.

FATHER: You might break it.

CHARLES: No, I will take good care of it.

FATHER: All right!  Here it is.  Bring it to me as soon as you find the top.

*(Exit Father R.)*

CHARLES: *(hunting again with light)* I should be able to find it soon with this light.  *(He hunts a moment or two longer).*  Ah! here it is!  I knew I should soon find it.  *(Stoops to pick up imaginary top).*  This will be a good story for Sister.  She can tell the boys and girls that they also need a light to find their sins.   But, father is waiting for his light.   I must bring it to him.

*(Exit R.)*

**Silent Reading.**  *Lightning.*

Before the story is read in class, divide the class into two groups.   Tell the children that different kinds of lightning have struck the story and left their marks there.   Tell them you want them to find how often each kind struck.   Words are bolts of lightning, and the number of times they occur in the sentence is the number of times the bolts struck.   The child that first finds the correct number scores a point for his group. Suggested words for this story are:

light—7; he—5; we—5; Charles—4; it—4; his—3.

**Related Stories from Other Sources.**

Our Lord shows that if the Jews give good things to their children, God will give the Spirit to His children that ask Him (St. Luke, xi, 13).

The Holy Ghost enlightened the Venerable Francis Mary Paul Libermann, a convert from Judaism, who later became a priest and the first Superior General of the united societies of the Holy Ghost, and of the Immaculate Heart of Mary.

Show the children that without the light of the Holy Ghost in examining our consciences we would act much like "The Blind Men and the Elephant" ("Fifty Famous Stories Retold," Baldwin), all of whom made egregious mistakes with regard to the appearance of the animal because they could only touch portions of his vast anatomy.

# TOPICAL INDEX

*Numbers refer to stories in Part One.*

www.ingramcontent.com/pod-product-compliance
Lightning Source LLC
Chambersburg PA
CBHW021046090426
42738CB00006B/216